DIARY OF
A HUMAN
LIE DETECTOR

Facial Expressions in
Love, Lust, and Lies

Annie Särnblad

ILLUSTRATIONS & BOOK DESIGN BY SARAH MATTERN
sarahmattern.com

STUDIO PHOTOGRAPHY BY BARRY BRAUNSTEIN
barrybraunsteinphotography.com

ISBN 979-8-9883819-0-7 (Paperback)
ISBN 979-8-9883819-2-1 (Hardback)
ISBN 979-8-9883819-3-8 (eBook)

To my Irreplaceables:
Emma, Rick, Carrington

In all my years across the oceans,
I never got over missing you.

Just as well.

"You love me out loud. I've never had that before."

"I will always love you out loud. It's the only way I know how to love," I answered firmly.

"Good. That's good, because I'm used to it now and don't want it to go away. Stay this time, Annie."

"I will, I'll stay."

These are all real conversations
I've had during the course of my life

my original intention was to mix
fact with fiction,
but it all came out true

because well,
screw it
life is what it is
blissful, loving, painful
and messy,
so messy

and emotions are taught best
when they are real

so here are some of mine

and this
is what they look like
on the face

Contents

Introduction | 1

 Love & Lust | 3

Crabbiness & Pride | 69

Kindness & Friendship | 99

Longing & Loss | 163

Lies & Betrayal | 181

Sadness & Struggle | 213

Fluster & Hope | 239

Introduction

For over a decade, I have taught facial expressions—the nonverbal and universal language of our species—to clients all over the globe, including Young Presidents Organization, Stanford University, NBC, The European House - Ambrosetti, and the Museum of Science in Boston. All my workshops and keynotes are interactive, and "learning by doing" is my favorite way to teach.

I have a peculiar brain, and though it's probably a strange thing to use my diary to teach emotion, my real work has never been far from my heart, my brain, and indeed my trauma. Emotion is taught best when it's real; so here is my own life, love, lust, and longing. Here also are some of the lies I've been told, along with how I've been able to identify them.

I hope the truth in my writing, prose, and verse will get you to feel emotions so strongly that you make the corresponding expressions on your own face. And that doing so helps you to absorb and learn as I pull these expressions apart, break them down, and teach you how to identify what each emotion looks like on the face.

This book includes plenty of repetition, as well as a **Facial Expressions Glossary** with clean and marked up photos of each expression so you can test yourself as you learn. By the time you finish reading, some of this should "stick," so you are left with words for things that you kind of, sort of, already know, deep in the subconscious parts of your brain.

All of the facial expressions I teach are universal and hardwired into us humans. They present on our faces regardless of age, gender, socialization, culture, and geographic location.

Facial expressions are a teachable skill because we humans have biological responses to each individual emotion. Each emotion creates a *specific* and *different* change in blood flow and muscle movement, in our bodies and on our faces. We are wired to respond to facial expressions when we see them.

There is a reason each feeling *feels* different.

We sweat when we are nervous, cry when we are sad, wrinkle our noses when we find something to be distasteful. When we are frightened, our hands get cold. Our lips tighten when we are angry. When we are sexually aroused, the blood pumps to the middle of our bodies. If arousal didn't lead to a change in blood flow and muscle movement, men wouldn't have erections.

Without erections, our species wouldn't have survived.

As you read this, keep a mirror or camera nearby. Read the descriptions of expressions and practice making them yourself on purpose in the mirror. Each emotion has its own primary locations in the body and on the face. I focus my teaching on the areas of the face where each expression is easiest to spot.

Facial expressions, especially the fleeting ones, show emotion and experience in their purest, truest, and most instantaneous form.

When you can read facial expressions, every face-to-face interaction with another person provides feedback. This feedback has changed the structure of my thought patterns in much the way that becoming fully multilingual has. It opens the door both to flexible thought and to seeing situations and humans exactly as they are, without a filter of translation. It also helps me learn what works and what doesn't when it comes to connecting with others and helping them solve their problems. Ultimately, it helps me to love well, and for this I am eternally grateful.

I hope by helping others to read expressions—and therefore emotions—correctly, we make the world a kinder, more connected, and more compassionate place for us all.

Indeed, it's harder to be crabby with other people when you can see that they are struggling.

Love & Lust

Pupils – Want, Desire, Greed

I turned to him and let my gaze rest on him.

"Oh God. Your pupils still dilate when you look at me."

"And that means?"

"Want."

"Oh." Quietly, "Yeah." Nod.

. . .

This is one of the most distinct memories in my lifetime, watching the man I love watch me. Finally and fully recognizing the depths of his desire in his swelling black pupils.

We humans dilate our pupils when we really, really want something.[1]

And he, he always wanted me.

He always
wanted
me.

Expectations

My profession isn't really to
grow your influence,
it's for connection, empathy and kindness,
so you are no longer blind to when
you hurt or heal someone else
my work isn't for the wallet,
it's for the soul

so, hold on tight,
it gets real, fast
and real can be scary
as you so know, my Love,
as you so know

· · ·

I often write my poems to "you." These stories span my entire life and the "you" represents various individuals. Some conversations are adjusted slightly to protect privacy, but even then, the gist of the story is true.

But yes, in the loving pieces, poems, and conversations, one man features in most of them, as he so knows. The entire language of human expression could have been written using only his face responding to me and mine.

He remains to this day deeply connected to my obsession with my profession, in that we both wished we were able to put words to what our hearts knew and our expressions showed so very many years ago.

Neither of us has ever fully recovered.

You

Y ou with
your lashes
and brows
lowering, relaxing your eyelids
dilating your pupils

looking at me with need and desire,
as if your soul wishes to reach into me and settle,
settle and stay

like it's entirely your right
indeed, my Love
indeed

remind me that
I live
I live
I live
risen again

*(Wait, maybe that's you. I always
did like getting a rise out of you.)*

• • •

Half-masting the upper eyelids is prominent in what we call "bedroom eyes."[2] This has a more intentional, focused, and hungry look than sleepy eyes, which give a groggy, blurred impression.

I watch TV sometimes with the sole intention of watching eyelids. This makes me weird. And also really good at what I do.

When you are unsure of a facial expression, imitate it—make it on your own face and sink into what it triggers in you. That is, after all, what facial expressions are for—they send messages to our brains to understand and feel—so we can interpret our emotions and the emotions of others.

---

2   See #31 in the Glossary.

Your Expressions

That's my favorite, you know. Of your expressions. The surprise and shock and awe all in one.

The complete drop and release of your jaw, as if you've simply forgotten to hold it shut. When I've said something stunningly ridiculous, not even plausible, and you realize as you work the puzzle in your brain that it must be true. And that it explains a lot about me, about us. That you didn't know. And wished you had.

Not that I don't like the desire on your face. The dilation of your pupils, the rise of your cheeks, when you half-mast your eyelids at me and tilt your head slightly to offer me your neck. But especially, when with it. Too. Is that piece of awe and surprise. Like you didn't expect to want me so much.

The pride on your chin I like, as well. Jutted forward, so as not to let your cheeks rise alone. In you, with that specific expression of pride, sometimes there is want. For me. Of me. In your swelling black pupils.

Your grief, I see, too. At times. In the pucker on your chin and the rectangularing of anguish in your lower lip.

Often directed at directions of ways, and ways of directions, and tunnels and dark places. Where you wished you could have done differently. Been softer with your words and actions. Done less or more. Seen the unseeable.

And your brain still processes these past transgressions. Of which, I know, I am but one. I see your mind works on the idea that maybe if we had been different, found a way through the woods, another set of dominos would have fallen. And your losses would have been less. Fewer. Not as devastating.

Softness and kindness and empathy, I find on your face too. In the rise of your cheeks with the soft pucker of your chin mirroring mine. And I know that you often hide your heart. These days, as well as those days. And when I see this and recognize it, and hold your gaze, your eyes get wet, as they are apt to when I am close.

Your anger is not my favorite. Unless, of course, once in a while, when I stand close to you and still feel far away. Then, I inspire the injustice myself, with a verbal poke or jab. And your frustration with me, the idea that I would underestimate you, flares like a rocket in your eyes. In the tightening of your brows and in the squeeze of your throat and vocal cords and lips. And I know. I KNOW. That if you are so crabby at such a little, little quip, then surely you must love me, want me, need me.

I know that it pushes the buttons of your feeling misunderstood, and that this goes back a long way in our lives. Which is why I shouldn't do it. And yet, I do.

Sometimes.

When I need to be reminded that you so want me to know you well.

I do, my Love.
I do.

• • •

This man is often sphynx-like with others, keeping his emotions close to the vest.

But with me, he surrenders, allows me to watch every fleeting emotion, stares deep into my eyes and tries earnestly to answer each question as completely as he can. Even the painful ones. His questions for me are thoughtful and endless: "Why and how and when did you know that you loved me?" "Why could you express the hard bits of your life to others and not to me when we were young?" "Why, with this connection, couldn't we make it work when we were young? Seven years, Annie. I asked you out for seven years!"

I'll pull apart these expressions more as the book progresses, but here are the basics of this piece:

Shock and surprise[3] involve a dropping of the jaw.

Awe, in this case, is approval and adoration shown in the lifting of his cheeks—I don't have a photo of this, as it's hard for me to recreate on demand like I can with most expressions.

Deep thinking,[4] or "working the puzzle," creates a furrowed brow—pushing the eyebrows together and down toward the nose. I get two vertical lines of wrinkles between my brows when I do this. I've shown this expression so often that you can see them etched into my skin even when my face is relaxed. We'll revisit this concept later.

Desire[5] is in his dilated pupils (that swell while we were talking), his lowered, flirty, bedroom eyelids, the joy in his cheeks when they rise and cause the skin under his lower eyelids to bulge out. The head tilt with other signs of desire show flirtation and a willingness to be vulnerable. There have been times when I've been with him that I get a neck ache from tilting my head so much. That's only ever happened with him. And because he knows me, and he loves me, I tell him that my neck hurts and why.

The neck tilt without all the other pieces can simply show affection, comfort, and willingness to be vulnerable with someone. I often do a quick, simple neck tilt with good friends, as well as with my kids.

---

3   See #28 in the Glossary.
4   See #2 in the Glossary.
5   See #31 in the Glossary.

His chin juts forward in **pride**[6] as he watches me, as he listens to me. I please him, and he is ever so proud of my brain and the woman I've become. His cheeks always rise in pleasure when he is proud of me.

His chin puckers in **vulnerability and tenderness.**[7] When the dimpled chin is part of tenderness or empathy or softness, it is usually accompanied by a soft cheek rise of joy.

When he shows **sadness,**[8] the pucker of his chin is also accompanied by a diagonalling of the skin over his eyelids.

When he expresses **grief and anguish,**[9] he twitches his lower lips out into the shape of a rectangle. Lip corners seemingly reaching for each respective shoulder. This accompanies the rising of the inner eyebrows of sadness and the raisiny, puckered chin of vulnerability.

And yup, sometimes I still piss him off. Often out of sheer neediness, immaturity, and, well, mischief. I get wiggly around him, especially when there are other people close by, and I feel needy for his attention. When I quip in salty ways, anger furrows his brow and tightens his lips and vocal cords. Sometimes he thinks I know him less well than I do. But I succeed in pressing his buttons spot-on, every time.

This is not particularly kind of me,
and I usually have to apologize.

---

6   See #24 in the Glossary.
7   See #29 in the Glossary.
8   See #27 in the Glossary.
9   See #23 in the Glossary.

A Handful of Boob

"Ohhhh, you are really wound up!"

"I'm fine. I'll be fine." Your words and your mouth, tight.

"No seriously, like really wound up. Crabby. Like a toddler who can't calm down without a snuggle nap and a handful of boob."

You threw your head back and howled with delight, then rested your face in mirth, "Where do you come up with this?"

"That's better. Now you look relieved and cheerful. Much better. Oh, I don't know. I just like to show off for you, I guess. I like your expressions of surprise. I feel like you're rarely surprised these days."

"Yeah. True," you silenced for a moment. "It's nice to be in middle age with you. I didn't like this age so much before. But with you, it's easier. In a lot of ways."

"Good. Me too." I smiled at you and felt my head tilt toward my right shoulder.

• • •

A **tight mouth** shows **anger.**[10] This makes sense as anger is a clench: clenched eyebrows, clenched lips, clenched fists, etc.

Mirth[11] is expressed in a slight downturn of both lip corners as the cheeks rise in delight.

A **head tilt**[12] can mean a few things, but *it usually means a willingness to be vulnerable.* I won't tilt my head unless I feel safe and comfort-

---

10   See #1 in the Glossary.
11   See #18 in the Glossary.
12   See #14 in the Glossary.

able with that person. I do head tilts all the time to show affection, tenderness, and most definitely romantic love.

In my life, so much of intimacy is created through humor. It's a balm and a relief, and it feels so very good. And just because someone is crabby doesn't mean we have to meet them with crabbiness of our own. Showing the opposite mood can sometimes pull them right out of their frustration, anger, or sorrow, especially if we know how to do it well.

Especially when they are easily influenced by and open to us. Especially when there is adoration, softness, and play in the relationship. In other words, when there is trust. And even if we only provide temporary relief, it still helps.

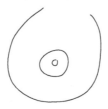

This is a picture of a boob.

It's in this book for the sole purpose of making my friend Marie O laugh. Also because she double-dog-dared me.

In My Clothes

" I like you in my clothes," he tells me, his gaze sweeping my body from head to toe. Sucking me into his swelling pupils.

I dip my head to the right. My ear to my shoulder, and I loosen my eyelids so they slip halfway down my irises. Pulling in one corner of my mouth to tuck it tightly into my cheek. My knowing smile.

My left hand pulls the sweatshirt from my neck up to my nose—to inhale his scent.

"It smells like you," I answer. My pupils dilating, as he lunges towards me.

• • •

I've noticed, as of late, that I let my eyelids drop down my irises when I **flirt**.[13] They drop straight down, as opposed to when I (or anyone else, for that matter) show sadness. In **sadness**,[14] the eyelids create a diagonal line with the outer corner at the lower end, sloping upward to the top of the nose.

When I speak of pupil dilation, I'm talking about the swelling of the pupils in the moment. They visibly become larger and take over the irises in response to a specific stimulus or situation. This occurs in **want**, in **desire**, and also in **greed**.[15] The dilation indicates arousal and excitement. As is the case with all emotions, what makes one person excited or aroused can be very different from what makes another person excited or aroused.

I've been told many times that chocolate dilates my pupils. Learn to pay attention to the size of the pupils of the person you are talking

---

13   See #6 and #31 in the Glossary.
14   See #27 in the Glossary.
15   See #32 in the Glossary.

to when you first begin a conversation. Pupils are different sizes according to the individual and the circumstances. We're looking for a change in size in response to the conversation and body language. Note when exactly they swell and try to figure out what the trigger is.

Sometimes it's in response to specific words and ideas ... and sometimes it's in response to you.

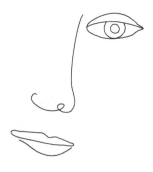

Humans are endlessly interesting.

She's Like Herpes

Y ou called
me herpes
to your client of all people,

you called me herpes
and I should probably be offended,
but instead I find it so deliciously funny,
deliciously *you*,
to be so unfiltered,
finally

it's how I like you best,
also it gives me something to poke at,
and I like that too

and yes, I am nearly impossible to get out of your heart
itchy, tricksy, love indeed

After I came off stage, you followed me like you did when we were young. This time, you were forced to wait for a line of men to ask their nervous questions, each speaking with a shy tucked chin, each asking sheepishly for a hug after I'd answered.

As the last man walked away, you stole the space at my side, tight into me like a child who hasn't yet understood or acquiesced to the appropriateness of bubbles of space. You were frustrated and flustered and *unsatisfied* with sharing my attention, as you expected to have it all to yourself.

I should have warned you that before I go onstage, I'm anonymous, but as I begin to speak, I become a magnet for needy souls.

One of your clients approached us, his cheeks lifted, pleased, his upper and lower eyelids slightly stretched extra open in excitement.

He said, "So let me get this straight, you've known each other for thirty years?"

"Forty," we deadpanned together.

"She's like herpes, you can't get rid of her!" Your words rushed out of your mouth, before your face froze in shock. You grabbed me with both hands and physically tucked my entire body into yours, as if hiding me in your armpit would make me, and your words, disappear.

*I do so love it
when you lose yourself
in me.*

• • •

Shock[16] opens the mouth, dropping the jaw. Sometimes it's a hard stretch, but in this scene, it wasn't. He just released his jaw, as if he wasn't able to remember to close it. He couldn't quite believe he'd lost his usual self-control. For me, it was pure victory. I have always loved that I move him, rattle him, make him feel and want and ache.

*So good to finally see you be you again.
Also, you are ridiculously funny, and more people should know that.*

*Corporate America sometimes takes good things away from good men.
Glad there is still some of you left for me to find.*

Our eyelids open slightly when we are **excited**,[17] and our eyebrows rise towards our hairlines. But if we exaggerate this too much—by pulling our upper eyelids way open—we look like we are signaling **fear**.[18] In the extreme, it looks like our eyes are bulging out.

16 See #28 in the Glossary.
17 See #4 in the Glossary.
18 See #5 in the Glossary.

I know a few people who are introverts who try to overcompensate for their shyness or sadness with a huge expression of excitement. It really doesn't work and often comes across as unsettling.

I believe this is why Hilary Clinton lost the US presidential election in 2016. It's just my speculation, but my guess is that she pulls her upper eyelids way back to try to show enthusiasm—when really this ends up sending a message of "danger, danger, danger!" This is the signal we receive when we see terror on someone's face.

I recently told a good friend not to over-open his eyes when presenting to clients.

"It's freaky," I said. "I know you are trying to feign enthusiasm when you don't feel it, but knock it off. Take a breath. You know your topic, and people like you. Don't overdo an attempt to connect."

He's sad these days though, so I understand why he would attempt to show enthusiasm, even when he can't muster it.

It's Funny

It's funny
how often
human beings fail to see things from
other people's perspectives
even ... especially
with the ones we love
particularly when we are young

and now, so many years later,
when I'm with you,
I can't not see your feelings fleeting
clear as daylight across your face
moving in your fingers, your posture,
slipping down your neck,
in the positioning of your head,
the swallowing in your Adam's apple
when I make you achy and desperate,
your body and pupils swelling
with want

• • •

I always watch for swallowing in moments of strong emotion. I see this particularly in men, so very much in those that are described by others as holding a constant, sphynx-like poker face. Not to me. *Not to me.*

The Adam's apple bobbing has become almost impossible for me to miss. When I see it, I quickly soften my words and actions to adjust to this demonstration of vulnerability. This swallowing movement shows when a man feels anxious, needy, or deeply touched.

When you are the only one to see emotion, you are the only one who can respond to it. With insight comes responsibility. I don't have any male friends or even longer-term clients who *don't* come to me with pieces of their lives that they need perspective and advice on. I take this seriously, and, if I can, I help them figure out how to be vulnerable and put words to their feelings so they can better share those emotions with their loved ones.

At times, I help men figure out how to talk to other men. But since most of the men I work with these days are from the US and in their forties and fifties, this is often hard. Our culture sometimes makes it difficult for men to be vulnerable with each other. I wish this were easier. I wish we were all kinder and softer with each other and better at understanding each other's perspectives and neediness. I often get asked what most surprised me after learning to read the emotions on people's faces. That's an easy question for me to answer:

Almost everyone is struggling and needy.

Bathroom Mirror

I remember seeing my face in the bathroom mirror of your parents' house. My skin flushed red from desire and endorphins.

And my cheeks, my neck, scraped from your five o'clock shadow. The almost black sand of your whiskers leaving lines and blotches of scarlet burn on my skin.

The balls of my cheeks rising in recognition of it, and one corner of my mouth tucked into my cheek. Happiness and satisfaction at the reveal, the evidence of your desire and lack of restraint. On my skin. On *me*.

The memory of which makes my breathing both deep and short. And shallow. Breath echoing in my head, right between the back of my nose and throat.

• • •

Romantic love on the face is a complex expression that I believe is almost impossible to fake. All of the pieces together build a paragraph of **romance** and **arousal**[19] that, when done right, is a combination of joy, vulnerability, softness, flirtation, and *want*. Because I can't fake the expression of romantic love, I've used my personal pictures in the Glossary. I remember exactly what I was feeling when these photos were taken.

These are the pieces of the expression of romantic love:

> Cheeks rise in **joy**, causing smile bags under the eyes.

> Head is tilted in softness and **vulnerability**.

> Chin is dimpled in **vulnerability** and **tenderness**.

> Eyelids are half-masted in **flirtation** and **arousal**.

> Pupils are dilated in **arousal**.

> Skin is often flushed in **arousal**.

> Sometimes you also see a **knowing smile**,[20] which is a soft, one-sided smile. When a knowing smile presents with the rest of these expressions, you get a look of extreme flirtation that says, "Come hither!"

---

19   See #15 and #16 in the Glossary.
20   See #6, #7, and #12 in the Glossary.

It Seems to Me

O ne of the sweetest things
I've ever read

was when a man with autism
confessed that his girlfriend,
whom he loved and didn't want to lose,
was upset because she felt he didn't show her enough affection

he said it wasn't a natural thing for him to think about
so, he decided, in secret, to treat her the way he treats the dog
thereafter, he would pet and scratch her when she walked by
and when she sat next to him on the sofa

it wasn't intuitive to him, so he created a recipe to follow
she's happy now, and he's hoping she won't figure out *his thinking*
and just appreciate the improvement

but it seems to me that
she's a lucky woman

because when she asked for what she needed to feel good,
he listened and he tried,
and he found a way to adjust to her

and that matters so very much, and is so very tender and kind
it seems to me

• • •

My clients with autism and my clients who are mathematicians have historically been my best students. I believe this is because of all the people I've worked with, these particular individuals have been extremely adept at *pattern recognition*.

Learn to see the PATTERNS and the MOVEMENTS of facial expressions, and you will improve your ability to see genuine emotions in real time on the faces of all the humans around you.

The really impactful thing is that it's easier not to be angry at other people when you can see their suffering. My children talk eloquently about managing crabby teenagers in high school. They say that the chin puckering[21] on an angry person's face serves to remind them that the person is struggling—making it so much easier to counter with kindness.

Growing up, my kids would say things like: *"Yeah, that girl is mad all the time, but she keeps squishing her chin into a raisin of sadness. So she's having a really hard time. I just asked her to join our group for lunch and now she's not so mean. I think she was just lonely. I asked her if she was doing okay, and it turns out her mom's sick ..."*

I do warn people, especially when I am working with their children and teenagers, that you can't ever unsee facial expressions once you've learned them. I remember feeling shocked when I piled my children into my car after having dinner with new friends and their children. I asked if they had a good time, since they had spent most of the evening running around with the other kids, and I had barely seen them. My ten-year-old daughter Lea said, "The kids were nice, but Mom, the parents are really struggling in their marriage." She had spent all of ten minutes in the same room as the parents.

I started working with my own kids on facial expressions before they were verbal. Most of the time, I think that's a good thing, and it has protected each of them at vital moments in their lives. And indeed it has helped them love and connect to others, but there are days when I feel guilty about the emotional burden they carry—seeing others' pain to the degree they do.

---

21 See #29 in the Glossary. The chin pucker shows vulnerability—and in this case that the person is sad and struggling.

The Naked Puritan

Naked. After the sauna. Running with my arms spread out high, holding the towel above my head so that the current of air pushes it up, up, like the cape of a superhero.

In the Swedish countryside.

Howling and hollering in delight, for the nudity, the rebellion. And the way your eyes rake over me.

Your cheeks rising high on your face. Your pupils dilated. Your head tilted to one shoulder.

"See," you told me in Swedish, "this is how I love you. Naked in all your glory. Free. Happy. Beautiful. Loved."

My overwhelming gratitude for your kindness, the depths of your joy in every piece of me ... for the softness in the way you loved me. Releasing me from the bands of my Puritanity.

Setting me up for a lifelong expectation of how a loved, adored woman should feel.

Especially when naked.

It helps.
Even now.
Especially now.

Tack snälla Du.

• • •

It's a *thing* when a man I'm in love with rakes his eyes over my body, as if inhaling me with his breath and his eyes, bit by bit by bit. I've been known to call this "the full body sweep." Interesting that if you're attracted to the person doing it, it's delightful, but it can be deeply unsettling if you are not.

Salty

I like both
your sweet
and your salty
so don't try to hide
your humanity
from me

All of It

I may
moan
and I may whimper,
I may even lose my temper

but Love, know this,
that you are to me
every single thing
I need you
to be

Weird and Wonky

Y ou can be
all weird and wonky
but know,
your weird and wonky
won't work with me

I know it's all anxiety
and you're not so big
and fierce
and strong

so, it would be better if you just said to me,
"I'm not feeling good, and I could use some help"

. . .

The older I get, the less patience I have for poised, polished, and pretend. I'm lucky that reading facial expressions means that I often have the choice to skip the small talk. I can always call out the expression on someone's face if I so choose.

Most of the people who know me don't try to hide how they are feeling, so we are able to talk about real, vulnerable things. Most of them express relief that I can read them so well and don't even try to pretend. And it goes both ways—I'm able to talk about my real stuff too. For me, this is simply a better, more meaningful way to live.

We humans need to feel seen to feel loved and valued.
Authentic and true is always interesting.

Unveil!

U nveil yourself!
      I told him
all of your armor:
let it fall down to your knees

clamoring!
banging!
groaning!

release!
until you are free
and can be with me who you
were as a child:
sweet, saucy, and soulful

I would have come back for you
you know,
all those years ago

I wanted to,
but your windows and doors were all locked tight
you had decided
that I was a harlot
and a betrayer of men

t'was not true
and also that's a weird way to view a woman
especially one you wanted
to bed, yourself

unveil!
and let the past lie in the past,
and be present here instead

(or be naked, naked also works)

• • •

With him, it takes me a good twenty minutes to get him to remember—
it's me. *It's me. I love you, and you don't have to show up as anyone
else. I love your flaws, and that you are silly, nerdy, and needy for me.
I worry that the world is losing you, and that I may be the only one
who is able to reach the pieces of you that aren't covered in armor.*

We humans only truly feel loved when we are seen with our flaws and
loved anyway. He has other good bits, but the vulnerable, the soft, the
doofusy in him moves and delights me.

And pretty much nothing pleases me more than making him stutter.

I Know You in Ways

I know you in ways
that are no longer knowable
I know you from
before you wore any of your armor,
from when you were still able to love
with utter abandon,
entire surrender,
as only a young child can

• • •

My friend B says that the best friends are the friends you make when you are in elementary school, before it ever even occurred to you to pretend to be anyone else. He says that you can't get away with faking anything with those old friends, and therefore you're always in the form of your purest self when you're with them.

One of my favorite things is when I get to see B with his best friend from the age of five. Two middle-aged men, each almost twice as tall as me, descending into fits of giggles and shenanigans. They always let me in on the jokes. And for a moment in time, every single thing in the world is good and only good.

This Lifelong Thing

I can
shut it off
with you

like I have done
so many times
before

close it
hide it
bury it

like I did
when we were little
and
when we were young

I could do it again
as a grown woman

but it occurs to me now
in the wisdom of age and experience
and knowing what I do
about life and love and humans

it occurs to me
that if I shut it off
I will lose
a good part of myself,
as well as a part that is good
that I am unwilling to be without

so I will leave the wound
open
undressed

even as you bandage and hide yours

as a grown woman
it is my prerogative

to live in the daylight
and let air and sunshine seep into me

even as I long for you
openly

knowing that even if I bury it
it still holds true

this lifelong thing
with you

. . .

When we humans repress our emotions and ourselves, eventually it causes **anguish**.[22] Emotionally, mentally, physically. My life is better, and I am healthier in all ways when I surrender to who I am, and to what I feel and know to be true.

Vulnerability[23] is most clearly seen on the chin—when the oval grape shape that is smooth and soft becomes a puckered, dimpled, cratered raisin. Try it in the mirror. If that doesn't work make the sound, "Awwwwwww," as if something is touching and tender. Try squeezing your chin a few times. Don't do it for too long or too many times at once—doing so sends the message to your brain that you are feeling the emotion you are showing on your face.

Vulnerability is a piece of the facial expressions of **sadness**,[24] **empathy** and **compassion**,[25] and love—both **affectionate love**[26] and **romantic**

---

22   See #23 in the Glossary.
23   See #29 in the Glossary.
24   See #27 in the Glossary.
25   See #3 in the Glossary. I view empathy and compassion as the same expression.
26   See #14 in the Glossary.

love.[27] If you think about it, this makes perfect sense. Vulnerability is the feeling of loss or pain or the *awareness of the possibility* of loss or pain. Anyone who becomes a parent is painfully aware of how suddenly sensitive they are in the world now that they love a child so profoundly.

Empathy and compassion, of course, have the feeling of shared difficulty or deep understanding of another's painful experience.

In my life, with this man, it's how I know, above and beyond his tender words and declarations of love, the true depths of his emotion for me. The slightest signal from me—whether it is of hurt or love or tenderness—and he responds, responds, responds. Chin squeeze, squeeze, squeeze. This, despite the fact that he is known for showing almost no emotion to others.

When he wears a beard, I can still see the movement that results from the chin squeeze—as it forces his lower lip up and slightly out.

I kind of, sort of, broke him when we were kids. He still loves me anyway. Telling him the whole story of our childhood and adolescence has been one of the hardest things I've done in my lifetime. For a very long time, he thought I'd betrayed him and that I never loved him back.

He's given me full permission to write about him, and he can't ever seem to get enough of what I write about us.

· · ·

"You don't have *more* ... that you wrote about me ... I mean *about me?*" He asked me not so long ago, with need and want in his voice.

I tucked my chin in embarrassment, then surrendered, "*They're almost all about you.*" I looked up at him through my lowered lashes, embarrassed and wanting. I watched as his furrowed, worried

---

27   See #14, #15, and #16 in the Glossary.

eyebrows smoothed and relaxed into their usual softer place. His cheeks rose high on his face, pulling up a wide, closed-lipped smile before he opened his mouth and let out a delighted laugh. He reached his grabby hands to pull the whole folder of my writings from me.

He was adjusting to this newly confessed, jointly acknowledged right of his, to read and reread all of my thoughts and feelings. My response to our mutual surrender that came so late in our lives when, at long last, the old and the new and the eternal meshed and melted and flowed.

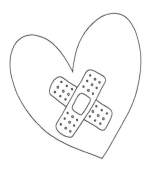

And he finally knew the truth,
that I'd loved him back,
the whole time,
all of the years
since we were children.

Oh Fuck!

"No no no no no, fuuuuck!"

"What?" He asks me, his hand still clutching the papers. He'd just read the rest of what I'd written about him, about us. My translation of his heart and mine. I'd watched him read, while I fiddled with my cold fingers, not knowing what to do with my body or face, feeling my every expression, in particular my quivery chin, as I saw his eyes darting over the papers, pooling with tears. His head tilted, his cheeks softly losing gravity as the seriousness, the real, and the passion of my writing overwhelmed him. As the whole truth flooded him.

"Oh no ... *I think you're my muse!*" I lament with whine and ache in my voice. I can't believe it, and it's all so very *tender and embarrassing.*

His laughter ringing, giggles rising up from his belly like bubbles of joy bursting out of his mouth, the loud noise in this quiet restaurant surprising him, astonishing us both. He stills, holds my gaze, his cheeks risen, his chin lifted, pleased and proud.

Oh no ...
I'll humiliate myself more ...
if it means getting this sound out of him,
getting this soft, happy, satisfied,
healed expression onto him
oh no no no no

but also

yes

also yes

. . .

He undoes me, this man. Just when I think I have all my shit together, a grown-ass woman, he does it again. This lifelong game of emotional ping-pong that our hearts can't help but play with one another. Because, in the end, it isn't a game. Despite the play, the banter, the poking, the pinching, and our "Bluff," it wasn't ever a game.

These are the expressions in this piece:

> The head tilts in a willingness to be **vulnerable.**[28]
> Chin puckers in **vulnerability.**[29]
> Chin lifts in **pride.**[30]
> Cheeks rise in **happiness.** [31]

---

28   See #14 in the Glossary.
29   See #29 in the Glossary.
30   See #24 in the Glossary.
31   See #11 in the Glossary.

"Expressions Math"

When I teach facial expressions, I focus on the location of the face where the expression is easiest to see.

However, because humans are complicated, we often feel more than one emotion at the same time.

So I teach my students how to identify when two or more emotions present simultaneously. Then we add them together and see what emotional "sentence" they make.

For example, if there is vulnerability on the chin, as well as a bit of joy from the rising cheeks, that's the more complicated emotion of **empathy, compassion,** or **kindness**.[32]

It makes sense in that the vulnerability on the chin in this context means, "I see your pain, I feel your pain." The joy in the cheeks, in this case, is actually showing "loving kindness" or an attempt to convey, "I hope it will get better for you." I make this face at my children all the time when they are sad or frustrated.

It's a bit complicated to get good at reading complex facial expressions. The different expressions layered on top of each other twist and pull and push the muscles—but the piece that is important to understand is to practice doing the "expressions math."

Think: one specific emotion + another specific emotion = what complex emotion? Voice it out loud and you can often figure it out. Also, remember to make the expression yourself. Your brain and gut will work at interpreting the signals for you.

Chin vulnerability + cheek joy = compassion, empathy, kindness

---

32   See #3 in the Glossary.

The Crease of Your Neck

I f heaven
had a smell,
it would be your skin
at the crease of your neck
and that smooth spot right below your ear

the sweet of your lips
as they reach
for me
pulling me, pulling me in

if heaven
had a scent
it would be
the crease of your neck,
the slight fold of the skin

where I push in my face
and breathe in
breathe in
breathe in

• • •

Lately, I've been talking with a loved one about the people in our lives who inspire a visceral response in us.

"He's in your cells," my friend told me about the man I love. "You've always had this really physical reaction to him. To his voice, his smell, his presence."

A visceral response can be equally as strong with a person who is toxic. I've stopped seeing and communicating with people who make me feel physically ill.

I'm not sure why it took me so long.

Love Through Laughter

It occurs to me
that one of the best ways
to love someone
is to make them laugh,

to shake them with love from the inside out,
tickle loose all the stress
so it rises up and frees itself

so, I will love you this way,
since it's my only path
my only avenue

and also because
I so love
your warm giggle

· · ·

"Not everyone gets to marry the right person," he told me, as his shoulders slumped, grief poured out of his cells, and his heart whispered to mine, *I love you, I love you, I love you. I love only you.*

Depression and sadness curl and tuck our bodies. We lose gravity and feel smaller. I think this is one of the reasons that hunching over to look at our electronics makes us feel bad—it sends messages to our brains that things are not going well for us. Our natural position when we are devastated is to curl into a ball. Sitting up straight tells our brains the opposite, that things will be okay. It's one of the many reasons I tell my kids that good posture is essential. Another reason is that when I lived in Singapore, the Aunties always said we need deep, good breaths to be healthy. Never underestimate the knowledge of the Aunties. They are protectors who pass along knowledge and wisdom and love from generation to generation.

Ball of Need

"You're a ball of need," I insisted.

"Not for other people. I'm not. I mean, I'm not needy for other people."

"But it's there," I pushed. "I see it, feel it, read it in your body and face and in the pulling strings between us that cover the length of the room. I feel you in the room before I find you with my eyes, you know."

He nodded tightly, not re-lifting his chin all the way up again. His head and eyelids seemingly surrendering to gravity. His pupils blurring slightly, losing their focus.

"I do," he said. "I know."

I have this thing with him. It stretches out, floating above all my research, all the training I've done with my children and students. There are pieces of it that I pull on, examine, fiddle with in my brain when I'm close to sleep or out walking. It resides permanently in my back, toward the middle part, below my shoulder blades. It aches and pulls and ignites when he's close. I feel him in a way I don't feel anyone else.

It may be why the words never quite satisfy or come out right, even though I search for them. Words necessitate a translation of something gray that resides deeper in the brain than the words can reach.

I know, as he does, that I am his key. He can't seem to let anyone else into the space I assumed and consumed so long ago.

This thing that we've only ever had with each other.

"You think," he told me recently, with a hitch in his voice and a stare as firm as I've seen in my lifetime, "that you'll connect with lots of people in your life. And then you don't." I watched the pain wash over his face in the rectangularing of grief in his lower lip, pulling its corners out and down toward their respective shoulders.

I knew what he meant. We found it so young with each other. Both terrified in our own way. Both differently devastated by the strength of the connection, both acting out against it. Trying to assert power where there was powerlessness, where there should have been surrender. Pride and fear and loss, because really it couldn't be *reasonable* to have this passion at such a young age. He watched me like he wanted to inhale me, merge with me, gobble and swallow me up. Like I would cure in him every ache, bruise, and scar. Satisfy every murmur of body and heart. He awoke in me things I wasn't possibly ready to feel. He tried to pull me in, asking me out over and over for seven years. He reacted to my rejections by seeking solace in the swift and shallow, and I was so hurt by his parade of girls that I closed myself off to dating entirely.

"This lifelong thing with you," I called it once. It would be forty years after we first met, forty years after we first loved each other, that he finally said, in words, "I love you." *Present tense.* And only after, I told him the whole story. Only after he flew to Boston to see me.

I know deep down that I'll be okay. I'll live fully and laugh often. I'm not sure he'll do as well. He looked defeated and exhausted a few months ago, the last time I rested my eyes on him.

And told him
goodbye.

• • •

He closes his eyes when he's overwhelmed by emotion. Momentarily, but it's one of the many ways he shows his feelings on his face.

There's a picture of me that he gave me that he saved for four decades. It's one of the ones he took around the time he first asked me out, in sixth grade. I'm embarrassed to show it here, but I carry it in my phone. It shows slight fear in my pulled-back eyelids, excitement in the widening of my lower eyelids, and dilated pupils from want.

I loved him, and he terrified me. Or more correctly, he was lovely and gentle and intense and all stuttery, needy boy. All lanky legs and thick, dark, sloped eyebrows and long lashes with sultry eyelids. *More correctly* ... my feelings for him terrified me.

He,

he

was

Lovely.

He is still lovely.

Surrender

R eal love always carries with it
an element of surrender
it took many, many years
before I knew,
before I fully
understood that

humans are so deeply messy and vulnerable and flawed
and yet
still capable of loving
the broken bits
in each other

Things Do Not Please Me

T hings
do not please me
I'd rather have
a poem
than a purse ...
a heart, a kiss
an "I oh so miss ... "

so gift me, Love,
the things of the soul,
that only fully sate
my palate
when they come
from you

Molasses

There
are times
when you are stuck
in the molasses of misery
and you need
a firm, swift pull
to yank you out of the muck
into the sunshine and warmth
and the remembrance
of who you really are

you did this for me, and someday, maybe,
you'll let me return the favor

(in the meantime, thank you)

• • •

I often think about loyalty and crisis. How when people help us when
we are low and down and small, we attach our hearts to theirs, and
stay, beautifully stuck.

Does He?

"So, I mean. Does he love me?" Her chin puckered and her eyebrows formed a triangle with the inside tips reaching up and toward each other. "I mean everybody must ask you this. I can't believe I am ... but, does he?"

"Oh. *So much.* You can see it in the way he lights up and his smile softens. His cheeks rise, he tilts his neck and puckers his chin. Vulnerability, adoration. You make him really happy." My voice was gravelly, and I felt the heat and sting around my eyes as I teared up. "It's good. It's really good."

...

Once in a while, I tilt my neck when I'm trying to tell if I like an outfit I'm wearing. But other than that, I only do it when I'm really comfortable and safe. I do it both with very good friends, some clients whom I both love and trust, with my children constantly ... and I also do it when I'm romantically attached to a man.

When it's combined with the lowering of the eyelids, pupil dilation, and softly, smoothly reaching up the hands to touch the skin on the face, the lips, and the neck, it becomes extremely sensual and highly **romantically charged.**[33]

Romantic or simply warm and **affectionate**[34]—a neck tilt is usually tender and soft.

---

33   See #15 and #16 in the Glossary.
34   See #14 in the Glossary.

What I Like

I like
the gravelly
in your voice
that you save
just for me
when you're sleepy and soft
and can't reach me all the way,
but your voice shows your
body's ache
for my heart
and my skin

• • •

I don't do much teaching about voice, as it's not my specialty. That said, I do pay attention to it, as I know it carries interesting information. I'm aware, for instance, that I'm more easily influenced by someone when they speak slowly, low, and deep in their throat. I have a friend who I'm convinced could get anyone to do anything with his smooth, comforting, convincing tone. He has the male version of a siren voice. He doesn't use it all the time, but it's a superpower he can pull out, as needed.

With the man in my poem above, it's the surrender in his voice that does it for me, his allowing me in past all of his armor. The intimacy in the way he uses his voice with me, even when we're in a public setting: he lowers it and it vibrates so that it feels like it's reaching into me. He watches me like a wolf when he does this, entirely aware of his magical effect on me. The hunger on his face is eventually accompanied by an expression of **mirth**,[35] a slight downturn of both lip corners as his cheeks rise in the delight of watching me respond and fluster.

---

35   See #18 in the Glossary.

The Reunion

Found and Lost Again

It had been almost 30 years since I had last seen him. I grabbed his hand and pulled, watching the recognition wash over his face. In his brow and chin. Eyebrows pulled first straight up in shock and then instantly more triangular, peaking at the center of his forehead. *Tenderness.* There, and on his puckered chin and slightly lifted cheeks.

So much time had passed.

My brows lifted horizontally, straight across my forehead and I, for a fraction of a second, wondered at this expression on my face, this one that even my well-versed brain failed to recognize. My irises as high in my eye aperture as they would go whilst still allowing sight. My cheeks lifting slightly.

My face's response to the unfiltered love and wonder he showed, his sheer vulnerability and softness. Open and needy. Waiting, cautiously.

I launched myself up and to him and squeezed him tightly, holding fast and steady, as he time after time released, loosened his grip, only to realize that I was refusing to relax mine. He surrendered and pressed me into him again. And again.

I am

found

and

lost again

(later ...)

"You give the best hugs," he breathed into my ear.

"Why? Because I launch myself at you and refuse to let go? You always did like the attention."

"From you, *yes*." He said, as I felt the wet from his tears on our pressed together cheeks, as he cried for us both.

• • •

Reading facial expressions means that in every interaction, I get instant, immediate, honest feedback. This changes everything. In the moment, I can pivot, soften, push, or pull back. Over the years, it means I have learned what works, what opens doors, what soothes and heals, what helps, and what harms.

Every

interaction

is

feedback

when you can read facial expressions.

Facial expressions, especially the fleeting ones, show emotion and experience in their purest, truest, most instantaneous form.

Chicago

I told him that I think of him every time I go to Chicago. And then I quickly followed with, "I almost never go to Chicago."

He thought it was a joke and burst out laughing.

And because I needed the relief, I joined him in the laughter. It was one of only a couple of times that he let his facade slip that night. With his carefully-crafted, professional questions about goals. To cover the ache.

But in his fatigue, he couldn't quite hold his mask steady.

• • •

I'm astonished by the sheer loneliness of many middle-aged men. To be fair, most of my clients are male CEOs or managing directors at the pinnacles of their careers. Many of them have chosen work over relationships and find themselves ever more disconnected and isolated as they rise in power.

And the skills that are currently valued in much of corporate America are often in direct opposition to the ones that are useful and effective in love. Kindness, willingness to adjust to others' needs and wants, openness of soul, honesty, clear communication, and vulnerability— are all so very necessary for true and lasting intimacy.

In addition, many of the salespeople I've worked with are experts at creating temporary intimacy. Very few are able to sustain it, and most of them complain bitterly about their marriages. How desperately sad to be the worst enemy of your own heart.

A client once confided in me that his best salespeople are those who are the most broken. "They need constant validation," he said. The new and shiny distracts them from their demons that pop up when it gets too quiet, too real. It also serves to distract them from their disappointed, heartbroken, and bitter spouses who couldn't possibly have the energy to constantly validate a spouse with a stunted capacity for emotional reciprocity.

Things won't love you back
work won't love you back
money won't love you back

only people
will love you back
and even then
only the right ones
whom you nurture
and love
well

(Thank you to my best friend, EFJ, for countless conversations about this, and about him, and for loving me back.)

Catching Up

For me,
love is often instant
or not at all
it's annoying to have to wait
for other mortals to catch up

I Dreamt

I dreamt
I put my hands up to your face
my thumbs in the indents of your smile,
and I said,
"someday my Love,
you'll wake up and
remember who you are"

Wake up

Wake up

Wake up!

Facial Expressions and Sex

" I 've been thinking about this, and I wish I could just say when I'm teaching that reading facial expressions is like being good at sex."

"Bah! Explain!" she ordered, her warm voice filled with mirth. I grinned, pleased to have surprised her.

"Ok. You don't have sex with a five-step plan—like some people run their meetings or run their pitches, barreling through with no alternative paths or courses of action.

"With sex, you have a general goal of—*ahem!*—what you want to achieve, where you want to end up. But you adjust according to the other person—because it's a *conversation* of two, not a monologue. Your responses, your rhythm, your movements depend on the other person's reactions and responses. A good lover doesn't just plow through ... "

"Bah! No, indeed. And that makes sense. You adjust, adjust, adjust to respond, to please, and also please and please! And then reach an outcome that is *mutually* satisfying," she added.

"Exactly! A good meeting should also include a plan of where you want to end up, but there should be adjusting along the way to the others' responses and reactions, with pre-planned options, so you can pivot if you see they absolutely love something in your pitch— or absolutely don't! Really, it's the same even for a spontaneous conversation. Give and take and respond! I have to figure out how I can explain this when I'm on stage teaching. I mean, without getting in trouble. That being good at facial expressions is like being good at sex—it means you're really into the two-way connection, and the other person feels that their *needs and wants* are seen and stimulated in a satisfying way."

"This is a good conversation."

"Right?!"

• • •

I'm endlessly grateful for the women in my life, particularly the old friends who process and think aloud with me. The best friends are the ones we can speak freely and unfiltered with.

Bantered and Bickered

W̶e bantered
      and bickered
and it thrilled me,
because we were so young,
and it was how I stayed connected to you,
and how I always saw
that I wound you up
more than anyone else

and that was so much better
than nothing

· · ·

I often think about the emotional resources (or lack thereof) that both
he and I had when we were young. I used to fight with him in school—
argue and say mean things to him. It was the only way I could manage
interacting with him, since being soft meant he would get emotionally
greedy for me and ask me out again. I didn't know how to be with him,
but still couldn't help pulling, pulling, pulling him in. For almost ever,
he thought he was alone in it, when he never, ever was.

It's not easy to be young and without emotional resources.

Surprise

"**N**o way. That cannot be true."

"Yep. It is." My voice softened, and I tilted my head. Looking up at him through my eyelashes and eyelids that had slipped halfway down my irises. "I never told you." Quietly, "I didn't want you to know."

"Wait ... so you?"

"Wasn't ever with anyone else. I didn't date anyone else. All those years." In my head I added, *I'm not a fickle woman. I know what and who I want.*

His jaw was slack, his mouth formed an oval "O"—the vertical wider than the horizontal. There was no stretch of the lips, as there would be in an "O" of excitement. I decided this was my favorite of his expressions. Open-mouthed, losing all muscle control in his face, so that his jaw fell down as his eyebrows rose up. Seemingly entirely of their own accord. Eyelids stretched slightly, a softer rise than in fear, instead of bulging eyeballs, just a gentle upwards pull of upper lids.

This boy, this man, who had taken evidence at face value, choosing ultimately to believe the words he heard over the expressions on my face. The concrete over what our souls both knew was irrefutable.

Kryptonite and fuuuuuuuuuuuuuuck,
I'm lost again
I'm still lost in you

• • •

A slack jaw shows **surprise**.[36] Surprise makes for a loose, round lower lip. I always think that the jaw looks like it suddenly forgets it's supposed to hold itself closed. It's a very satisfying expression to inspire. Addicting, in fact.

---

36   See #28 in the Glossary.

Did I Tell You?

I think, I said,
I thought I knew
all the things I'd say to you
but when I got there,
all was gone

when all is said and all is done,
I wish that I had been the one
to love you all your days,
in so many, many ways

I wish I said
the things I thought
all the words that I did dread
I wish that I had said them all
back then so you would know
I love you so

More Than

I like you
a little bit more
than I'm comfortable with
so can you please
be patient with me?

Not Unrelated

"It's not unrelated, you know," I told him suddenly. Rushing with my words to offer him as many bits and pieces as I could. Knowing there wasn't much time left in the evening, and thinking then that I likely wouldn't see him again. (I would. He would make sure of it.)

"What is not unrelated?" he asked, boldly holding my gaze while trying not to drown in the intimacy of it.

"My obsession with the nonverbal, it isn't unrelated to us. What we went through, put each other through when we were young. I didn't mean to hurt you. I was broken. I'm so sorry." My mouth tightened, puckered, both movements pulling in the corners of my lips. My chin squeezed and forced my bottom lip to protrude slightly.

"I, um ... thank you." Reserved, measured, keeping the physical space between us in a way he had never before. And yet his eyes. Soft and open. And despite his body's attempt to hold the distance steady between us, he mirrored my every movement with his own, betraying his resolve. *This*, I think to myself.

This. I've never seen in all of my days, ever.

Oh, *Sweetheart*.

Down to his fingers. I move my fingers, and, as if there are invisible strings between us, his own twitch. I remove one from my cheek so only two remain. He does the same.

"Down to my fingers," I hum.

"What? Your fingers?"

"Down to my three fingers, on my cheek. These." I wiggle them. "You mirror me down to my fingers ... "

"And this means ... " He knew. I was sure he knew.

His needy eyes yanking me in, with just as much force as they used to. Only me now with no armor. Not even a thin layer over my heart. Just years that vanished. Adult brains, gazing on open, raw, teenage hearts.

"It means affinity. Connection. In our case, we're aligned, connected. There's love."

"Mmmm." His eyebrows raised, daring me to see the attached souls, the sadness, the closeness, and the distance.

I see

I know

Still

. . .

Among the pictures he kept of me, there is one of us together when he was still eleven and I had just turned twelve. Over the years I had grieved that I didn't have a single picture of us—and only us—together. He had one and carefully saved it.

The positioning of the upper body matters less in body language than that of the knees and feet. The upper body is often positioned in opposition to genuine intention. We seem to be more aware of what our upper body is doing, so we're more able to control the message it sends out—making sure we're socially appropriate. We seem to be less cognizant of the positioning of our legs and feet. They're much sneakier.

The positioning of my one knee in this photograph kills me. It betrays my resolve, not only because of the exact mirroring of my knee and his, but also because it's showing that I'm opening up to him in the same way he is to me.

Back When

You were the only one
who could keep up
intellectually,
go toe-to-toe
with me, back then

the banter
was glorious,
back when you
were unfiltered,
and magnificent,
and terrifyingly
real

back when you were present and *with* me,
it felt like bathing in sunlight

back, when you still *lived*

Old Pair of Jeans

"I like spending time with you."

Silence.

"Me too," I whispered.

"You look the same."

"Ha, do not."

"No, really. You look exactly the same as when you were twenty. You haven't changed." His face was soft, his pupils round and swollen with blurry edges, and his right ear leaned slightly toward his right shoulder, exposing his neck. I looked at the two even holes in his beard under each side of his lower lip and wondered whether my fingers or thumbs would fit more perfectly into the shapes.

I pulled and tucked the left side of my lips into my cheek. My knowing smile.

"Ahh, I'm your old pair of jeans," I said softly, looking up at him through my lashes, my eyelids relaxed and slipping straight down over my hazel irises.

"Excuse me?" His formality leaked over our comfort.

"The jeans that you loved, that looked amazing the first time you bought them, tried them on. You looked hot. And as the years wore on, and the jeans wore out, your stomach sticks out over the waist, giving you muffin top, and they sag a bit in the butt. But you still think they look the same. And your family members shake their heads, because they see that the jeans really don't look great. But, no matter. You're still convinced they do. You think they are the best. That's me. Your old jeans."

Softly, low in his throat, "I did love those jeans." His cheeks relaxed and seemingly moved to the side and slightly upward.

And into the night he fled.

I leaned back and sighed.

Kryptonite

and

Oh

lost again

· · ·

So much of love is blind once the attachment is deep. Our species should be more grateful and more aware of this. It's a gift. Well, *mostly*.

When teaching, I make a point to clearly differentiate between the **knowing smile**[37] and the **sinister knowing smile**.[38] The knowing smile — the *Mona Lisa* one — is just one corner of the lips tucked in tight to one side. A knowing smile is devoid of malice and has no movement of the nasolabial fold (which is the line from the outer corner of the lip up to the top of the nostril). If that line is deepened, the expression shows malice instead of softness and has an element of sinister arrogance — the sinister knowing smile.

I particularly look for this sinister expression often coupled with deep disgust—which looks like a dog snarling or growling—when I'm protecting children and assessing who they must be kept away from.

Always look for the nostril shadows. If these shadows are present, that means there is a piece of the **NO Face**[39] and an indication of disgust and/or discomfort.

---

37 See #12 in the Glossary.
38 See #13 in the Glossary.
39 See #19 in the Glossary.

Sexuality, the Swedish Way

Giggling at your rendition of the class you substituted for. In that Swedish high school, instructing sexuality to these young men, barely younger than us.

And you, in all your Swedishness, taking the responsibility seriously. Important to be clear, to instruct. To make them comfortable in their humanity, in understanding their own bodies and their partner's pleasure.

My laughter as you recounted their questions. They had asked you seriously, as Swedes are apt to do. About your girlfriend. About what we did and what women liked. You blushed when you repeated the conversation to me, having refused to answer those questions.

Instead, asking me to help you to plan for the next lesson—so that it would come, also, from a woman's perspective. And my reply: it seems that the education, the honesty, will serve them well.

In life, and in love.

"Tell them this and this, and to do this before that. Not to do this, unless she asks. And this, this way, only. Tell them that he should give her at least one orgasm before he enters her, and let her come down from it for a few seconds so she's completely relaxed when he does enter. And to try letting her set the rhythm once he's inside, if he wants her to entirely surrender to love. And orgasm together with him. That piece is important for him to understand, because she won't always know how much it matters that he not move too fast until she catches up, and even if she does understand this, it can be hard to ask for."

"What about *this*?" You ask.

"Mmm, Ja, definitely that as well," I answer with my knowing smile, the left corner of my mouth tucked into my cheek that lifts it slightly. My one-sided, warm smile.

Your earnestness and intention were pure. Your laughter and joy in the conversation, and at my willingness to put it all into words, after being so shy with you in the beginning of our relationship.

I think of you sometimes. And your untimely, early death. Because of my constant moving, I only learned of it so many years later.

• • •

This is slightly fictionalized in that I added to the story the advice I wished I'd been given about sex when I was a young woman. My then-boyfriend didn't teach those pieces, but he did ask me what he should tell his students from a woman's perspective. I remember how thoughtful he was, as Swedes so often are. He was a good man, and he died way too young.

Remember that the **knowing smile**[40] has no nostril shadow (which would turn it into a **sinister knowing smile**[41]). It's just one side of the lip corners tucked into the cheek with sometimes a light lift of the cheek on that side. It's often soft and warm. Like the gentle holding of a secret.

---

40   See #12 in the Glossary.
41   See #13 in the Glossary.

Origin Story

"**O**h, God. You're my origin story."

"Your origin story?"

"Yes. Where it all started. That's *sooooo* awkward."

"Why is it awkward?"

"Ugh, it makes me all wiggly and uncomfortable. This shouldn't be a public thing."

"Then just don't make it public."

"I can't. There's always a price to pay for having a superpower. You're mine. And the vulnerability. Surrendering to it. I can't talk about needy, messy humans without exposing myself … Can't teach what faces, expressions look like without using my own face and my own heart to show it.

Otherwise, it's just not genuine.

And then what is even the point?"

• • •

Holding back[42] is the facial expression that puffs out the skin under the lower lip. It looks almost as if someone has tucked a piece of chewing gum between the lower teeth and lip. It takes a lot of muscles to make this movement and it's an expression that says, "I have something I want to say, but I have a reason *not* to say it. I want to say it *so badly* that I have to physically restrain myself from letting the words spill out."

I first saw this expression on the face of a loved one when she was being mom-splained—and incorrectly so, but nevertheless with enthusiasm and conviction.

42　See #9 in the Glossary.

In work, I teach my clients that if they see someone make this facial expression in a meeting, they should pull the person aside later to follow up. Since the person making this expression was so clearly itching to comment on something, they will in all likelihood tell you what they are thinking if you ask a question such as, "Hey, when the topic of X came up, you looked like you had something to say?" Or a less direct approach: "How do you feel about X?"

Point being, people who make this expression usually have a strong opinion that for one reason or another they are deciding not to share in a specific context or group. Barack Obama is the king of this expression. This makes sense when you think about how often he must hear someone say something he doesn't agree with, and decide that this isn't the time or place to voice those thoughts. Self-restraint is a good quality in a leader ...

Crabbiness & Pride

Taut and Crabby

Y ou forget whom you speak to,
  forget what I know
convenient perhaps,
so please, have a go

I will correct you,
with bliss and with savvy
I remember things most
when I'm taut and/or crabby

• • •

Anger,[43] **deep thinking,**[44] and **working a puzzle** all involve a scrunch of the eyebrows.

I have two lines that look like parentheses on my glabella, the skin between my eyebrows, but on some faces, only one deep wrinkle appears. Even when my face is "flat," neutral, and expressionless, traces of these vertical lines remain visible between my eyebrows.

Neither my children nor I slept well when they were little. So these particular lines on my face are from years of trying to problem solve how we could all get more sleep. The lines that are etched into our faces show our life experiences—or more exactly, how we emotionally responded to those experiences.

For example, constant **distrust and discontent**[45] leave deep wrinkles next to the nostrils. Repetitive **joy**[46] instead leaves deep wrinkles like parentheses outside both lip corners.

---

43   See #1 in the Glossary.
44   See #2 in the Glossary.
45   See #20 in the Glossary.
46   See #11 in the Glossary.

I find this to be one of the many things that lets me know how to quickly connect with a stranger in front of me. It shows me what I'm "working with." It also helps me manage people who are crabby—I can instantly recognize from the placement of their wrinkles that their emotional state has everything to do with their life experiences and very little to do with me. I often see it as a challenge to break the shell of emotional protection with kindness, warmth, insight, or laughter. Most eggshells can be cracked, but please remember that if you crack them open on purpose, you should also try to care for the gooey, leaky, emotional insides. Try not to make a mess if you aren't going to help clean it up.

The way to tell if a person is showing anger rather than just trying to figure out or solve something is that an expression of anger will have tight lips. Whether the mouth is open, pouted, or closed, the lips will be *tight* rather than soft and relaxed.

On a side note, different languages also leave distinct lines on the face. I can often tell, for example, if a person of a certain age is likely to be a French speaker or a Swedish speaker if I see vertical lines above the center of the top lip running upward to the nose. Both of these languages pucker the mouths of their fluent speakers, eventually causing wrinkles to be etched into the skin from the repetitive movement.

No Good Hugs

You forgot
my birthday again

so, since I'm tired and cranky
and disappointed again
and because I don't like feeling that
you're the boss of my emotions ...

from now on, you will no longer get my good hugs,
the ones you say are the absolute best hugs
of all the hugs in your life,
the ones that make you feel loved and wanted and whole

you may have the clearance section of the big-box-store hugs,
the mediocre,
bumpy,
flimsy,
loose,
emotionally empty,
sad hugs,
the "wet fish of handshakes" hugs

henceforth, you are relegated to these
for the rest of our lives
because,
as it turns out,
I'm still petty

and you still insist
on hurting my feelings,
even though I asked you not to

• • •

I can't tell you how many relationships I've seen where one person opted out by ignoring the other person and their needs and wants, even after it was communicated clearly that this behavior hurts. Messages are unreturned. Well wishes or checking up on someone when they are lonely, sad, or sick never come. Promised visits never happen—and aren't communicated about, because doing so would be uncomfortable.

Fine, if that's really how you feel, but ... entitled, ill-mannered, and so very foolish if you do actually love the other person.

In our case, he leaked and foreshadowed my not talking to him in the future. I believe he was sabotaging us because he was scared.

I watched his expressions when it sunk in, what he had done. The multitude of times he ghosted me or took me for granted and assumed he'd have another chance ... at some later time.

He was so devastatingly surprised when he finally realized that treating me this way was a surefire way to remove my option to stay. In any capacity at all.

I'm just as proud as you are.

Doofus

The Massage

I wrote a
crabby poem
in my head,
when I was getting a massage,
but I lost it,
couldn't access it in that grumpy part of my brain
that was rubbed away by skilled
fingers and hands, that seemed to find
and loosen every knot of pain,
both physical
and emotional

I'm not sure I still want it,
since bliss feels better
maybe I'll go back and get another massage
to see if I can find it ...

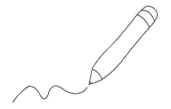

For Loving, Not Using

I'm not for using.

I'm for loving. For tenderness and adoration and surrender. For laughter, but not the haha kind, the bubbles-up-from-your-tummy kind, found in sheer joy.

I'm for loving. Filling your heart and making your soul sing. For giving you a home in me. And for seeing you entirely, flaws and demons and broken shards of glass in your solar plexus. Release it all into me and find in my skin, solace for all that ails you. I'm for healing and for both now and eternal.

I'm for loving, not for using.

You misunderstood me
completely.

When We Met

Your friend
told you when we met
not to pursue me,

because despite the palpable connection
between you and me,
I was already sleeping with someone else

the "other man" of
whom your friend speaks,
is wired and wound,
a hugely heartbroken human,

if I were sleeping with him,
he'd be happy and relaxed,
his soul soothed, his body sated

he is neither of these things,
and there within
the proof

He Knows About Me

He knows this about me,
that I often think
I'm the smartest person in the room
it's because
my particular form of intelligence
is attached to my survival

so, he needs to be able to manage that,
and pull the red balloon back down,
when it starts to float away

which can be a lot to ask of a man,
who is entirely consumed by his own pain

• • •

So much of bravado and ego is a defensive response. I'm always taken aback when someone assumes that a big ego is a sign of self-confidence. In my experience, it's usually the opposite—the ego is a cover for massive insecurity.

The obsession with power comes so often from a feeling of powerlessness. Usually, the person has been let down, bullied, or even abused. Often there has been a long period of their lives when they felt unloved.

I have had many male clients and friends who feel safe enough to take off their masks with me, to show how desperate they are for tenderness, kindness, and compassion. There is a deep fear among so many humans that if we are known fully, we couldn't possibly be loved.

So the Swedish "evil circle," or what we call in English *the snowball effect*, rolls on. Tenderness comes so rarely to those who are boisterous, big, and bullying.

When someone trusts me, they can often respond well to my "knock it off and be kinder" pushback. Firm words. "You know you are okay. You don't have to try so hard. Listen a bit more." Also, soft hugs and gentle words can go a long way when there is trust and connection.

It's not hard to be kind, to tell someone the real things that you appreciate about them. They will recognize the truth.

Fitting

I belong
a little bit
everywhere
and a lot
nowhere

Still

You are grieving
still
I know that
but your full-on commitment
to misery, to stuck
both at home and at work
doesn't work for you or for me,
so I'm letting go

let me know if you want to come to
where the river meets the rain
and live, live, live
because time is running thin

*and I'm still in
this thing
with you*

Unconditionally, Apparently

" I love you. I will always love you!"
you spat out angrily into my calm

and I realize looking back,
that I didn't reciprocate, that time
didn't say, "I love you too"

it is at least something,
this fiery reaction
the one we've always
elicited from each other

you still turn me upside down
and inside out
good
that I do the same for you

and yes, most definitely, indeed
I still love you too,
even when you are drenched in and
dripping with crabbiness

some things
do last
a lifetime,
at least,
thank God for that

Going Rogue

"I'm going rogue," I told her.
"No man, no person, will longer rule over me.
I'll write with all that I've come to be

and if those who've wronged me care to see
my writing,
then they will also have to look inside themselves,
or simply put down
the fucking book,

because this is mine.
and they have no right to the narrative
I write about my own life."

"Amen to that," she said. "I'm right here beside you."

"I know," I said. "It's pretty much the best thing in the world.
And as I tell you almost every day, I love, love, love you so."

My narrative.
My life.

Acquiescing

B ecause love
is acquiescing,
adjusting,
accommodating,
to at least sometimes
meet in the middle
and I always did
and you never did
you asked me why,
and that's why

The Foreigner and the Alien

I 'm ever the foreigner,
never completely belonging
anywhere in this world,
but you're the alien,
the from-another-planet man,
who can't even speak
the language
of Love

Tarzan

I t's how you love me, Doofus
it's one of the most necessary,
primitive, biological pieces of courtship
between a man and a woman—
that at least sometimes,
you let me talk you into things

things that take energy, or risk pride,
or make you feel vulnerable
it's ultimately what *feels* like it would keep me
and my offspring alive,
your willingness to prioritize me
is necessary to woo me
it always was

if you won't let me feel like I have
even the tiniest bit of influence over you,
your willingness to give me
even this small victory,
I will feel unloved and undervalued
and have *no idea* that you care for me

to deny me is to reject me

my sexuality, my openness of body and soul,
is dependent on feeling safe and adored

also you could have sent me that funny picture
of you dressed as Tarzan
I wasn't feeling well,
and laughter would have helped

it shouldn't be so hard to remember to choose kind

turn your heart back on,
you've been sleeping for far too long

. . .

Trauma seems to make people freeze and impairs flexible problem solving. One of the most important pieces of love is faith. Faith in the other, faith in oneself, faith in love. And for me, faith in God.

Vulnerability requires trust that we can show our weaknesses, and they won't be exploited or thrown back at us.

The Martyr Who Walked into the Sea

He was fearless as a child,
now shriveled as a man,
half the height and half the width
and all, "I don't think I can!"

how sad to see for us who love him,
this once Majestic Beast,
determined now to lick his wounds,
and so deny the feast

• • •

I see so many "ambitious" men in the middle of their lives who have seemingly reached their goals and who are so unbearably sad. So desperately lonely. I'm not sure if their relationships failed and therefore financial success, power, and status became more prioritized, or if prioritizing work over relationships made enduring intimacy all but impossible. Either way, it doesn't seem to be working out.

Sometimes, middle-of-life presents the opportunity to find clarity. But it must be seized and worked at. Growth rarely comes without struggle.

Intimacy necessitates vulnerability. We can't feel close to others without opening up ourselves. Unfortunately, corporate America still mostly frowns upon vulnerability and sees it as weakness. When truly, vulnerability and tenderness can be utterly majestic and form the strings that bind humans to each other.

It's particularly painful to spend time with someone you care deeply for and not be able to reach them.

In my life, I've watched many of the women close to me take back their power in the middle years of their lives. Friend after friend has begun to better assert their needs and firmly take up more space. To me, this seems to be more of a midlife awakening than a midlife crisis. More of a *midlife clarity* and a conscious awareness of the limited time we have left. "Hurry, hurry, wake up," so many of us seem to be saying, in words and in action:

"Wake up,

wake up,

and live!"

My Compatriots

I purposely scared them off,
these compatriots of mine,
who knew nothing of the trauma
of my younger years

I did it as a way to weed out the weak
whack out the weeds
weed out the whacks

funny, that the best weapon
in the war on Love,
is just to be a little too clingy

"needy" takes care of the problem
of too much attention right away,
silly and predictable, but Oh, so effective

besides,
it never worked on Viking men,
which is interesting

they'd simply hold my gaze
and call me out on my bullshit,
every time

and I'd wonder:
how did they learn to do that?

• • •

Ah, the Swedes, who are simply so well versed and comfortable in the parts of their humanity that I was so deeply uncomfortable with. Thank God we humans are resilient and can learn new things. And thank goodness for kindness, empathy, and understanding.

And growth. Thank God for growth.

Do You Remember?

D o you remember the period
for about six months
around seventh or eighth grade
when you decided you were going to become
proficient at winking?

I'm still traumatized

• • •

(Not really, but kind of, in that I still freak out if a man winks at me.
And no, I don't really know why, just that it has something to do with
you. Argh, for imprinting!)

The Yucky Man

The yucky man thinks
he knows about people
but all he ever sees is reflections of his own image:
hall of mirrors
hall of mirrors
hall of mirrors

• • •

It seems to me that the more selfish and deviant a man is, the more he's convinced that everyone else is awful in the same ways he is. Projection, projection, projection. This man is particularly creepy, he leaks bad intentions everywhere. Those who pay attention see it in him.

I do love my profession and my skills, but you don't need to know the vocabulary and building blocks of facial expressions in order for your brain to receive messages about someone's intentions. Please trust your gut when your brain tells you someone is sinister. I could always tell—long, long before I knew how to dissect facial expressions and put them into words. Long before I could read the science of sleaze, I knew when someone was "off."

Stay away from people who fleetingly get that dead look in their gaze. At best they are traumatized, at worst extremely dangerous. Don't stick around to investigate.

Run!

No Space for Small

There is no space
in my life
for small-hearted humans
that is all
that is all

Well Played

You played
and we both lost
because it wasn't a game
to me

Your Plan

So your plan
is just to be crabby until you die?
this is the dumbest, stooooopidest
most foolish of all the plans ever

choose love, choose big
choose real
choose life with me

now and now and
now
even if being happy is so ridiculously
scary
to you

Unkind

Not sure
how it came to be
that you were so unkind to me
consider yourself dismissed

I Think

A woman appreciates a man
faking his love for her
about as much as a
man appreciates a woman
faking her orgasm

both are disrespectful
and treat the other as puny,
powerless,
and pathetic

that sucks,
and not in the good way

Control Preferences

"Argh, you must have seen what a shit show that was. When all the people in the room have control issues. ALL. OF. THEM. Including you and me."

My daughter was finally old enough to take the wheel and was happily driving us both home from what I considered a stressful event. I was exhausted by the performance of appeasing too many people at once. She, on the other hand, was pleased with the sheer quantity of facial expressions and much less sensitive to the audience. She loved what I liked to call "the full carnival of emotions."

"Nope, I don't have control issues. PREFERENCES. I have control *preferences*. And my *preference* is to have control. And that's not a problem. Control *preferences*, Mama. Leadership skills. We have control preferences. This is a good thing. Strong and capable is good, Mom."

I glanced over at my child, growing up so quickly, and indeed knew that her power was phenomenal already. She had caught her first predator at the age of five. She was all soul and mischief and empathy. Her fierce need to protect poured into the marrow of her bones at a tender age. No wonder. *My* child. I often fretted over whether the skills I had instilled in her as a toddler gave her more joy or more despair. Both. It must be both.

Her chin was set, pushed forward in pride. Her cheeks risen in delight, squishing the skin under her eyes into smile bags. The muscles upon which her eyebrows rested pulled down and together towards her nose.

She would live her life. She would play and love and work. All the while, I wondered if she would always be pulled back to the lifelong work we did together. That she absorbed like a sponge. The vocabulary of emotions that she had been gifted, that had been shoved into her arms, into her heart, and into her soul, like it or not, in a not undesperate attempt to keep her safer than I was. I hoped she wouldn't inherit my need to run. That she would be grounded and find a home.

Like her brother and sister, she had been trained to see every single emotion in the person she was looking at—in the exact moment these emotions presented—on each and every face. Even the slightest flicker of a facial expression couldn't escape her. Even if it was unknowable to the person expressing it.

Her original and universal human language—the one that almost every other human banished into their subconscious—remained entirely intact and permanently accessible to her. At the stage of toddlerhood, where most humans push it away or have it pulled away, in favor of socially accepted eye contact and facial expressions, hers were acknowledged, strengthened, identified, and analyzed.

Instead of my native English, we used our Swedish to narrate the faces, body language, word choice, and behavior we observed in daily life during our many years in Singapore. Secret conversations, live, in-person, watching, analyzing—out loud—the humans around us. On buses, in schools, restaurants, grocery stores, at the doctor's office, in the street. Over and over.

"What do you see? What else? What does she do when he does that? How about now? Why? Why do you think she moves away?"

"Mama, she shows dislike when he moves toward her, into her space."

"How do you see that? Where on the face? Where in the body? What about now?"

"Disgust next to the nose and contempt, the lip pulls up into the cheek, Mama. She *doesn't* like what he said."

"And when that boy there moves, what does that girl do?"

"She moves closer."

"Why is that interesting? What is she feeling, and what do you imagine she's thinking? *Why?*"

Not only could she see it, but we began to notice that our shared vocabulary was evolving. Simplifying the pattern recognition, putting it into words that work to teach both very young children and much older multitasking CEOs.

Observation → Assessment → Insight → Strategy

Strategy built on correct assessment. My kids heard me say over and over again, "To get the strategy right, you have to build on what is really true. It's impossible to help, heal, and soothe humans if you don't understand them and their situation correctly."

See and pivot,
poke and prod,
see more,
pivot more.

Love
Protect
Heal

. . .

These are the expressions in this piece:

> Chin thrusts forward in **pride**.[47]
> Cheeks rise in **joy**.[48]
> Eyebrows furrow, pulling down and together in **deep thinking**.[49]

---

47 See #24 in the Glossary.
48 See #11 in the Glossary.
49 See #2 in the Glossary.

Butcher, Baker, Banker, Wanker, Wanker, Wanker

U gh for the married men in flux who think it's a good idea to hit on me just because there's no ring on *my* finger ...

I will listen to your words and listen to your face until you get all the way through your pitch.

The answer is no
no, no, and no
if you don't love your wife, divorce her
set her free
surely *she* can do better

That said, thank you for donating your facial expressions to my research. The seduction pitch hasn't been decoded quite so efficiently on the face until now.

So there's that. And well, I guess, thank you for your "business" even if it is only silly business.

Here are some quotes from married men I've met in life and work—since my divorce. In exactly zero of these cases have I been introduced to the woman they casually and callously refer to as "the wife."

"I'd love to moderate you ... if that's what we're going to call it. I mean, wait ... are we talking about the same thing?"

"I was aroused—at our first meeting in my office. I was aroused."

"DIRTY BITCH" *(um, predator much?)*

"Erections for you? All the time ... "

"Can I just ask you ... I'm married ... but if I wasn't, would I have a shot? A guy like me? With you? Would you give me a shot?"

"You have beautiful breasts, no seriously, they are beautiful."
(Obviously, he had never seen them.)

"Have you ever been with a [man like me]? Seriously. The one thing you need to know about us is that we are pleasers."

"Can you just send me one dirty picture?"

"can I Get a VISuaL?"

"Oh yeah, my marriage is over, we're still roommates though" (?!)

"I HAVEN'T HAD SEX IN OVER A YEAR—THAT'S BAD RIGHT?! I MEAN, TECHNICALLY I'M MARRIED, BUT AT WHAT POINT DOES IT NOT COUNT ...?"

"My therapist says I have to wait until the eighth date to have sex. The women start complaining, though, and try to negotiate to get it earlier." (This one was single and wasn't hitting on me—his expressions and banter were entertaining on a day when laughter was particularly welcome.)

"MY WIFE AND I HAVE A GOOD FRIENDSHIP. IT'S NOT A ROMANTIC RELATIONSHIP, THOUGH. HASN'T BEEN IN A LONG TIME. I DON'T BELIEVE IN THIS WHOLE SOULMATE THING, I MEAN WE CAN LOVE MULTIPLE PEOPLE ... RIGHT?"

Me: "No, nope, no way, not!"

. . .

I sometimes get asked if I would ever work one full-time job. Not if I can help it. The main reason I work for myself is so that I can maintain the ability to fire my clients or choose not to take on further work. There are a multitude of reasons to move on, in addition to inappropriateness, of course. There are so many good men in the world, men who respect and care for their families, their friends, and their colleagues. Men who support and lift others up when they have the chance. I'd rather work with the men and women who want to make things better for other people.

I'm lucky to have that option.

Kindness & Friendship

Depends

" A re you sleeping?" I asked him.
"Depends," he answered, "On how much you need me."
"Sleep," I told him. "We'll talk tomorrow."

Oh for boys
with all the right answers
for making me weepy and needy
when I wasn't

• • •

Some people seem to have a natural ability to see others for who they truly are. We can't feel entirely loved and cared for unless we are seen and understood. But even with people who are gifted at reading others, creating lasting intimacy means we still need to be brave enough to show ourselves to feel seen and loved.

My friend and I have a name for the phenomenon where someone feels that their romantic partner should automatically know what's going on inside their heads, without any communication.

"The game where everybody loses:
Guess What's Inside My Head?"

It's so much more effective just to tell the person you love what your needs and wants are.

That said, it's lovely when someone knows you well enough to intuit what you need. In my life, that hasn't generally been found in family or romantic relationships, it's mostly been good friends. One of my cousins is extra good at this. She looks at me and just sees me. I am grateful.

I'll Translate

"I'll translate it for you." I told her.

"Translate? What do you mean?"

"Translate the unsaid in our meetings. Facial expressions are our original language. Some people can hear it, or in this case see it, but they don't know how to articulate what they see. We've talked about your intuition, how you can often see the big picture of the expression, but you can't break it down so that we can talk about it. You lack the vocabulary to describe the pieces of it. Put it in context. I'll teach you."

"I can't do what you do, Annie. But I am good at reading people. I feel like I can really tell in my gut what someone else is feeling. Even if I can't quite explain it. I like it when you break it down and explain it. I feel like I kind of already knew it, even if I didn't have the words."

"That makes sense, particularly because of the trauma you experienced as a child. You couldn't afford to forget the skills of your primitive brain. When I teach, what I'm doing is connecting the primitive, the subconscious, to the conscious brain. The reason people can learn it quickly and are able to say, 'Ah, yes,' is because their subconscious recognizes it from when they were itty bitty. The things you knew when you were preverbal.

Most babies look all over your face to see clues for emotions, scan-scan-scan, track-track-track, side-to-side, level by level. But then, at some point in our development, we lose this ability. Maybe we are trained out of it, maybe we just don't feel we need it once the verbal language takes over. Regardless of why, we stop seeing many of the clues of facial expressions when we begin to favor eye contact.

Each emotion has its own primary locations on the face. I teach the pieces that are clearest to see, and I view it like building with Legos. Add the emotions that present on the face together, and they form for you the sentences of our unspoken, universal language.

The true language of our species. I'll teach you what I know, so you can see it too.

But beware: what's seen can never be unseen.

It's a superpower, this X-ray vision."

The good,
the bad,
the evil
and the achingly
soulful and kind.

Juicy Bits

"You know," she said to me, "this is the most honest, intimate relationship I've ever had. I've never felt like this. Like I can tell you anything. You won't judge. You might laugh, you might challenge, and *God knows* you'll tell me if I'm wrong. But I've never had *this*. Not with a man or a woman. I wish we were gay, and we could get married. I'm just not that attracted to you that way though. No offense."

"None taken," I answered her. "I'm only attracted to men, so that wouldn't work for me. But here's the thing. Why *wouldn't* you tell me the real stuff? The juicy bits? They are the interesting parts of life. The pieces to dissect, to analyze, and to laugh at. Humanity is funny. Sooo *funny*. And interesting. And *JUICY*."

I continued, "Of course, you are traumatized, with what you have endured. How could you not have trust issues? And while I ache for what you've been through, I'm beyond impressed that you have risen. That you use your powers for good, I mean mostly. Only once in a while for trickery. And then only if it's intoxicatingly funny and doesn't hurt anyone's feelings.

And you trust me because we recognize each other. Superheroes always have an origin story birthed in pain. As do villains. It's what you decide to do with it that defines you. You make a decision to be either all about protecting others or all about protecting the self, at the expense and sacrifice of others. Selfless or selfish. It's your fierceness in caring for others that distinguishes you. Makes you sooo interesting. And the fleeing, the running. I do it too. Doesn't mean I won't come back. If I'm anchored."

"I'll be your anchor," she said. "You can run when you panic. Because let's face it, we know we will. But promise me you'll always come back? Also, remember I would jump on a plane to get you.

I would come for you. They wouldn't, I don't think. So, if it ever comes down to it. *Choose me.* Now that I've started telling you these things. These thoughts, I can't stop. I don't want to. I didn't know it could be like this. And I want to tell you my stories at the end of the day. Like a cat delivering a mouse, I want to impress you. Mull it over with you, giggle with you about it. I'm a feral cat, you know."

• • •

There is no intimacy without vulnerability. And although this piece is about friendship, healthy, lasting, romantic love also necessitates vulnerability.

I've been thinking a lot about people who are able to create vulnerability with others. Some of them create and sustain it. But I've also watched many people, especially over the last couple of years, who can only manage intimacy for short periods before retreating and pretending it never happened.

Then they create intimacy successfully with a new romantic interest or even a client during a sales pitch, but they panic when it becomes real. They run, only to begin the cycle again with a new person.

Point being, be mindful of whether or not a person can maintain the intimacy they participate in. The ability to face and manage conflict is necessary for deep and permanent connection. If the individual is conflict avoidant, long-term intimacy will likely remain elusive, unless they get help managing their problems.

Real love always carries with it the possibility of loss. Anyone who's ever had a child knows this on a deep, primitive level. It's why I always look for the puckered chin of vulnerability[50] to see if a person is deeply attached to me. The man I love puckers his chin in a physical response, showing that he feels what I feel, every time I express my own vulnerability. It's one of the many ways I know that he loves me.

---

50   See #29 in the Glossary.

Emotional Legos and Location

"And do you like your work now?" I asked her.

"Yes, it's good." She sighed. "I needed to get away from the risk. I'm not all-the-way an entrepreneur like you."

She tightened the muscles in her chin, pulling it in and up, giving the entire oval of it small dimpling craters.

"Your sweet, vulnerable chin says otherwise. I mean, that you aren't comfortable with your work. That the change makes you sad."

"Oh. You can see all that on my chin?" Chin squeeze again.

"Yes, right there." My fingers touched her chin, softly. "Right here. See, I automatically mirror it on my own chin. I can see when you flash it. At the very moment you mention something. Or at the moment I say something. It shows vulnerability in response to the verbal trigger. The squeeze of your chin comes before the thought process. So you can't hide it. I can't even hide it on my own face. With all of my years of training, I can't hide it.

"It's usually interpreted as 'sad,' but really it's vulnerability. It's a piece of sadness, but also a piece of compassion, empathy, and love. Very much in romantic love. Especially. Which makes sense. It's like Legos. Each emotion has a different primary place on the face. If you know the locations, it's easier not to miss the emotion. The flicker takes place in different LOCATIONS. And you can build a sentence of emotion with the Lego pieces of each individual emotion."

"Oh. I guess I can't hide anything from you."

"Why would you want to? Our souls always understood each other. I won't ever judge. I admire you and the heart you put into every piece of your life. I know you live with guilt. But you shouldn't, you shouldn't. You don't deserve that. And you're a good mother and a good friend, and you shouldn't ever feel small. It's a thing you know. Us women. No matter what we do, or how we love, or what we achieve, most of us feel small. A lot of the time. You've always lifted me up. When we lived on the other side of the world."

So good to see you, my friend. To steal away this moment in time. Just for us.

• • •

Remember that **vulnerability**[51] is found on the chin—the relaxed chin looks like a grape and the puckered, vulnerable chin turns that grape into a raisin. Another way to think about it is "puckered like the craters of the moon."

---

51 See #29 in the Glossary.

Gentle

"**O**CD," he said quietly. "It means I'm really clean."

I threw my head back, laughter pouring out from my tummy.

"That. That's the funniest pick-up line ever." Then I smiled softly and held his gaze, looking up through my eyelashes at his needy, tented eyebrows and puckered chin.

"Ok, we'll walk around the puddles," I said.

He grinned, pleased with himself for making me laugh, and pleased with me for the gentle understanding.

Abilities

The ability to talk grown men into silly business is a hugely underappreciated talent.

"So *poppycock* is my word of the day. I'm going to say it a lot today. Double-dog dare you to say it in one of your meetings!"

"You're on. I'll use it multiple times."

"And report back?"

"Obviously."

(hours later)

"You did it?"

"Ha, of course. Did you doubt me?"

"And?"

"Got some strange looks and some muffled giggles."

"HA! Good. Giggles are helpful, especially in boring meetings. *Cockamamie* is a good word too ... Oh. Um ... this may be a theme..."

• • •

This is a conversation with one of my favorite clients. The laughter is a release and is connected to both of our abilities to access the extremely creative and strategic parts of our brains. In every interaction with him, I make him laugh within the first few minutes. It completely changes his ability to focus on the meeting at hand, with me. We talk openly about this. I even say to him, *"and now you are with me"* when I see the focus and intensity replace the jittery distractedness he arrived with.

Facial expressions are my constant teacher: what works, what lands, how the person is feeling, what they need, and what they can give to others.

adjust, pivot, learn, repeat

The Real Story

The real story
that I don't tell is that when we met again,
you followed me like a puppy, and I was torn
between the thrill of being wanted by you,
and the panic of being wanted by you

I could read expressions by then,
so the arousal in your pupils,
the tenderness in your puckered chin,
the affection in your closed-lipped, risen-cheeked smile
wasn't something I could even pretend not to see

every time you joked,
even when we were surrounded by others,
you met my gaze to see if it landed,
to bask in our connection
amused and aroused and relishing in my laughter
"get your pupils under control," I told you,
in mirth and in pleasure

you grinned, when I called you out,
as you are well-acquainted with my superpowers
you so graciously gifted me the full view of your emotions
not even attempting to mask them

when I started to feel overwhelmed
and told you that I needed to drive back,
you stuttered and stared at my mouth
before saying an awkward, "well, goodnight then,"
even though it was sunny and mid-day

I could have cried,
I was so touched
by the way
I moved you

. . .

These are the expressions in this piece:

> **Arousal**[52] is in the dilation of the pupils—look for the swell of the pupils *in the moment.*

> **Vulnerability** and **tenderness**[53] are in the puckering of the chin.

> **Affection**[54] is in the lifting of the cheeks that gently pull up the corners of a closed mouth.

> **Mirth**[55] is in the rise of the cheeks with a slight downturn of both lip corners.

When we are genuinely moved by someone, we are rarely smooth. This man sometimes stutters when he talks to me. It touches me deeply that I make him nervous. He is a brilliant and powerful man, but to me, he's an old friend who more than once stopped a family member from hurting me as a child. I am so very grateful that he saw me and protected me during a time in my life when I was very young and felt invisible.

As an adult, it's always interesting to me that people will often follow the lead of the person who is most formal. I do not. My children tease me that I have such problems with authority that I can't even follow a recipe without changing the ingredients.

I also enjoy the mischief of trying something that seems hard for others. What happens if you expect me to do this, and I instead say or try *that*?

---

52 See #32 in the Glossary.
53 See #29 in the Glossary.
54 See #14 in the Glossary.
55 See #18 in the Glossary.

That said, when the stakes are high, and certainly when I'm in negotiation or protection mode, I behave and am highly alert—always ready to adjust and pivot. But when the stakes are low, I experiment with my words. My willingness to test and try, poke, prod, and provoke means that I get constant feedback on humans that other people don't. Seeing minute facial expressions also means I get instant information on whether I've gone too far—so I can immediately pull back and soften. I believe this is why I've advanced so substantially in my abilities to recognize human behavioral patterns. Assessing a situation or conversation as it's happening is important. But even more important is knowing how to fix it. In other words, getting the assessment right and then building an intelligent strategy based on the correct assessment. If we get the assessment of the situation wrong, the strategy will also be wrong. This is true in any interaction with humans—in business, friendship, romance, parenting, teaching ...

Get the Assessment Right ——to——> Get the Strategy Right

And going back to the formality piece, it is hard for one human to stay formal if the other refuses to match their formality. Especially when the person poking has the advantage of knowing the other person for a very long time.

This man is one of two men I've known well going all the way back to our childhoods in Glencoe, Illinois. Today, both are extremely polished and poised, to the point of being almost emotionless in business and in social contexts.

I will have none of it. It feels boring and dumb and lonely and sad.

I've been asked how I can crack these stiff men, why they are warm and emotionally soft and even giggly around me. Both of these grown men cry when they are with me, sometimes tearing up in public. I think this is one of the greatest gifts I have been given in life—that I'm able to reach people and make them feel safe enough to feel. That these men who trust very few people are able to believe that I love them. When I see the emotional surrender and relief wash over them, tenderness and joy wash over me.

I think I can sometimes reach aloof people, especially ones I know well because I refuse to let them lead. I joke and am soft and affectionate with them when few others would dare. A big bear hug, gentle teasing, terms of endearment. And simply saying, "I'm so happy to see you!" I really, really am. People recognize the truth when you put it into words. And the truth is, I'm so eternally grateful to both of these boys (now men) for the kindness they showed me as a child, when kindness felt rare to me. My turn now to return the favor.

We humans recognize the truth when we see it.

Sometimes social rules are dumb. Sometimes it is hard and lonely to be in the middle stages of life.

Sometimes when you are big and powerful and everyone wants something from you, you just wish for the relief of spending time with someone who loves you for you. So you can lay bare the soft, nerdy, and sweet in your less-than-smooth childhood self. The most real and tender parts of you.

Body Before Brain

"Annie, the thing is, and I want your perspective ... The guy I was telling you about, the one I ended things with. The first thing that happened is that I stopped wanting to have sex, like before I realized that I wanted it to be over. I guess thinking about it, that kind of happened with all my other relationships too. I stopped wanting the guy in bed. Just got tired of the sex."

"You mean before your brain noticed how irritating he was."

"Yes, exactly."

"That's so interesting, that your body knew first, before your brain and heart knew."

"Yes, that's it—my body just said, '*Nope, done.*'"

"That's like my work with facial expressions—the expression comes before the feeling is processed and understood. *Always.* The facial expression, *the flicker of facial expression*, comes first. Before the brain even comprehends the feeling.

When I'm tired, I know to just obey my face, and I don't even bother with my brain. So, yeah, knowing and trusting my face, I get lazy sometimes, I guess. I register the expression with the emotion that it represents, but I don't always try too hard to figure out the why of it if I'm really tired. And I'm good with saving some nuggets to chew on and think about later when I'm more relaxed. On my walks or on train rides or in hot showers—I reprocess and relive why a specific conversation or event caused discomfort, vulnerability, or anger to flicker on my face."

"Hold on. Wait. So you mean you can feel it on your face as you're making the expressions?"

"Yes, absolutely. It's a learned skill, but yes, I pretty much feel every single one at this point. It's not my profession, it's my obsession. Trauma and survival response scraped into me, branded on my insides. It's my effort to control the chaos of the world around me and, well, stay connected to my subconscious, which I see as my safety mechanism. I can't shut it off. The recognition of facial expressions as they pop up—it's like Swedish and English for you and me. Both languages are ingrained so well that we can't switch either off.

So if two people are talking at the same time, one in each language, you and I hear them both, understand and process both people, both languages, all of what they are saying. We can even replay it back afterward. It's the same thing. *Multitasking.* My face doesn't shut off, it's like an additional language talking to me, telling me clearly what my subconscious knows for sure. All day long and at night too.

I freeze my face often when I wake up from dreams. That way the expression stays still so I can dissect it and pull it apart—even if it's multiple feelings and multiple expressions overlapping and pulling on each other simultaneously. We humans don't always feel just one emotion at a time—we can be sad and angry and resigned all at the same time. But if one of the emotions you're feeling pulls skin up and the other pulls it in the opposite direction, the result has a different manifestation than only the one expression ... I'll demonstrate when I see you. My own face is my best research."

"Oh fuck, that's a lot."

"Yeah."

. . .

I use my **NO Face**[56] to decide whether to buy a dress or go out with a man. If I look at the dress and wrinkle my nose—it's actually more of a quick flicker on the side of my nose—I'll never use the dress.

And, well, if I want to know definitively if I'm romantically interested in a man, I think of him naked. If I flicker my NO Face, it's a firm no. I know from experience that will never change.

Love and attraction are instant for me ... or not at all. The same is true for platonic relationships. I know instantly if someone is one of my people. Someday maybe my brain will figure out what it is that I see, smell, or feel that gives me the ability to know.

Kindness

" Y ou have a home with us,"
     he told me
she nodded, in unison,
in compassion and in friendship

"if you need to run,
you have a place to go,
a place to write
there's wine and paper and peace,
in the archipelago,
where the soft Swedish words
whistle
and the water laps at the shore

it's yours whenever you need it,
the red house
by the sea"

---

56   See #19 in the Glossary.

My Humanity is Lovely

I like my humanity
nothing else
in me
is real

I like it,
no apologies for that
I like the soft and the bulges
and the wrinkles on my face
that are me

and so does everyone else
who loves me

• • •

My client and friend Rebekah Barr calls the skin that bulges under the lower eyelids when the cheeks rise in **joy**, "smile bags."[57]

We humans love smile bags. Plastic, poised, and polished feel unsettling to our brains, hearts, and souls.

---

57   See #11 in the Glossary.

The Boy with Many, Many Things

As he showed me all of his things like a needy child at show-and-tell:

"I'm building a big house, on big land. Another one. In addition to the castle I already own.

And cars and planes
and art I have.
And I have a string instrument with a name. It's the only one."

He looked me in the eyes
and on my face,
scanning to see,
willing me to acknowledge.

At the instrument, I threw my head back, laughter bellowing out of my tummy.

"Of course, you did. Of course, you bought it!" The naming of it somehow making this funny to me.

He paused for a second, furrowed his brow, pulling the muscles underneath his eyebrows down and together, forcing the skin on his glabella to deepen his two vertical lines of worry. Mine clearly wasn't the usual response to his "exhibiting."

But then again, the list of his accomplishments and things came out so fast, so deliberately, so needy. This time.

He watched me laugh. Moved his eyes down to my vibrating chest. And then he surrendered. As if laughter this free had been forgotten. Realized he was caught. Remembered, and saw me clearly once again. The little girl from his childhood. His sister's friend.

He joined me, a grown man submitting to his own giggles. I watched the relief wash through his body. "Oh. *Oh.* I'd forgotten," his heart seemed to say, "we were connected before all of this."

My heart whispered loudly to his, "Your things mean nothing, but even before your acquisitions, your brain was a sight, your humor a balm. Your sensitivity as a child touched me. You were quick to feel hurt. That piece is gone now."

The man is broad and firm and peppered with gray. And it will likely be a long time until we meet again.

Your things mean nothing. But the way you hold my gaze … The pucker of vulnerability on your chin … The neediness pressed out when you slope your eyebrows into a triangle on your forehead, hoping so desperately that I will approve of your words, approve of you.

I do.
I have so missed your soul.
Be well, my old friend,
be well.

. . .

Deep thinking,[58] or figuring something out, creates a furrowed brow from the pulling of the eyebrows together and down toward the nose. This expression makes two vertical lines of wrinkles on the skin between the eyebrows on most people, but every once in a while, I'll notice that a specific individual only gets one vertical line.

A **sad**[59] expression makes the eyebrows pull up in the middle of the forehead to form a triangle. The skin underneath the eyebrows collapses and often makes a diagonal line from the outside corners of the eyes up toward the top of the nose bridge. This is one of the only expressions I can't make on demand, so there isn't a perfect picture in the glossary. That said, if you truly hurt my feelings, my face will make this expression perfectly. A full sad expression includes the puckered chin of vulnerability.

Vulnerability[60] squeezes the chin and turns the smooth oval part of the chin (that I liken to a grape)—into a squeezed raisiny-looking chin full of tiny dents and craters.

---

58   See #2 in the Glossary.
59   See #27 in the Glossary.
60   See #29 in the Glossary.

They Can't See What They Don't See

He understands
better than most men
that fragility and fierceness
go hand-in-hand
in me

"in order to do your work, you need a thick skin," I told him,
"and in order to do mine, I need to stay vulnerable,

I can't stay in your environment
and remain soft and kind
your cave of business
eats the souls of its dwellers
I do love working with you
but I can't stay

this isn't a natural
habitat for me,
the ice and stone
chill my bones"

"then we go," he said,
"we leave in the dark of night,
the real work is just beginning,
they'll never notice we left,

they can't see what they don't see,
they can't see what we see,
soul sister of mine"

. . .

I talk about reading facial expressions as my superpower, but those
who know me well, know that that's only the half of it.

My superpower is in the combination of reading the emotional state of the person in front of me—instantly and at all times—AND knowing what to do with this information.

Before moving back to the US, before I was public about my ability to read facial expressions, I spent almost two decades doing strategic advisory across Europe and Asia. Sitting in on high-stakes negotiations and working with CEOs, management teams, and boards. My human-reading skills were known only to a handful of close allies.

In work, in politics, as well as in our personal lives, it's fundamentally important to assess a *situation correctly*. But then, THEN, we also need to know what to DO about that situation.

1. Assess the situation — correctly
2. Know what to do
3. Do it

My strength is knowing what works with and for humans.

It's knowing how to soothe and encourage,
strategize and inspire.
How to help
and how to love well.
How to love well.

When I'm stuck in a situation where I can't love well, where relationships are transactional rather than reciprocal, then I know it's time to plan my exit.

A Nap, a Snuggle, and a Snack

I often get asked
why I'm comfortable with people in power
even the first time we meet

there seems to me a correlation,
that the more polished, poised,
and plastic a person is on the outside,
the more bruised, battered, and broken
they are on the inside

if we understand that big, powerful men
are just little humans in big bodies
like all the rest of us

only more lonely
and more removed
from real and authentic

then it makes sense that
they are often
in dire need of

a nap
a snuggle and
a snack

we big humans are still little humans on the inside

· · ·

So yes, I find men in power to be some of the easiest people to get along
with. I think this is partly because, to me, they tend to be predictable,
and partly because they often respond well to real, insightful, and
intellectual. And to someone who fearlessly speaks the truth to them.

I find I can usually get them to relax more quickly than most other people when they understand what I do for work.

I do write a lot about men specifically. Maybe that's because I find women so much easier to intuitively understand. But certainly, it's also because most of my clients are men. Also, in this piece, I say "men" since, in my experience, women in power tend to have and maintain more connection and affection in their lives. This doesn't mean that we don't often need a nap, a snuggle, and a snack too. Indeed, we do.

The Bear

When I got divorced,
he messaged me in the morning
and at night

day after day,
night after night,
having been through
it himself

and knowing
that it's the "good mornings" and the "good nights"
that are terribly missed
having someone
to say things to

the habit of having a person
a little thing, perhaps it could be,
except that he was across the sea
from me

and so, it meant everything that he kept track of my time,
kept track of me

until it wasn't so hard
anymore

Kindred

"It's because you're everybody's therapist," my friend said to me as he topped up my wine glass before refilling his own.

"Yes," I nodded once, emphatically, relieved that he intuited the secrets of my work. The things I couldn't, shouldn't, and wasn't allowed to say.

Relieved that he saw pieces of me that were invisible to others.

I had read this same recognition on his face the first time we met. Saw it instantly, in the pucker of his chin, in the diagonal folding of the skin attached to the outer corners of his eyelids, slanting up toward his brows. I felt it in the length of his gaze. The way he held my eyes in his, with grief, different from the needy, insistent way other men lingered in a long stare. This was a knowing, fully grasping look.

A wordless paragraph of pain.

The empathy pricked on his chin, so clearly birthed in his own history. He was someone who hadn't been able to banish his infant instincts to a remote corner of his subconscious brain. No, these instincts were instead sharpened, polished, tended to.

Kept, always at the ready.

"You tell me your things, too," I protested. He was as attached as the others.

"Yes, but you lean on me back. You also lean on me."

My chin fell in a nod that landed on my chest and stayed there. My eyes down. I surrendered, "Yes." How unusual for me to lean. But he was right. I couldn't help it. This man who had been to hell and back. Who had clawed his own way out. Who still caught demons by the throat, and beat them, most of the time. Who understands on a visceral level, as do I, that the world is a dangerous place and evil walks among us.

Ultimately, I just knew in my bones,
that I could rest while he was in the room.
Catch my breath,
let someone else stand guard,
if only for a moment.

• • •

These are the expressions in this piece:

> His **knowing** was in the tuck of his left lip corner into his cheek.[61]

> His **sadness** was in the diagonal fold of the skin above his eyelids.[62]

> His **tenderness** was in the pucker of his chin.[63]

> His **understanding** was in the length of his gaze, which so clearly voiced:

"I've got you.
I'll step in if you need me to.
I don't know you.
But also,
I do."

---

61 See #12 in the Glossary.
62 See #27 in the Glossary.
63 See #29 in the Glossary.

I've Never

"**I**'ve never," she told me. He told me. They told me. "Felt like this. What is it even?"

"Mmmm. Honesty? Intimacy? Connection? *Real?*" I asked.

"Like I need to tell you everything, you witch. These things that are so private. That I thought I was alone in. And you shrug, you normalize, you see."

"Well, it's not like they are *really* weird. These things that we all feel. We love someone we shouldn't, or don't love someone we should. We're angry and disappointed, sometimes abused, and often underappreciated. We're lonely and scared and we pretend we're not. We stuff our lives with stuff to fill voids. We sleep with too many people, or too few, during our lifetimes. Or simply, not the right ones.

We sometimes don't dare to say we love someone when we get the chance. And that ache, that loss. It sticks and pokes when we least expect it ... And not in a good way." *Grin.*

"Yes. Ok. But why am I telling *You?*"

"Because I made you laugh, and I told you some of *My* things. I was honest and open, and you could hardly. Hardly, hardly wait.

For someone to see you. And for someone to love you as you are. With all of your flaws and kindness, mischief and grief. I see it all on you.

It's a thing. We humans need the emotional snuggle. And the physical hug at the end of it all.

Everyone has a thing. This is mine. I see people. And love them through their grief.

Besides, I'm broken too."

. . .

So often in my life, new people express surprise at why they suddenly find themselves divulging things to me that they don't tell anyone else. But I find it easy to help people share their worries because I see the needy, pained, vulnerable expressions of loneliness and frustration. All it takes is a tiny opening, a willingness from my side to be real and vulnerable, and they can't wait to express themselves to someone who will listen without judgment and help them to solve complicated people problems, if they do indeed want solutions. Sometimes all they need is an ear.

The trick is to jump into the cold water first. To be the first to leap and lead the way, and then wait kindly with a grin to see if they will follow.

I Hope, He Said

"I hope my friends know, Annie, I'd show up for the big things. I'm not good at the little things. But for the big things, I'll come," he wrote to me.

I paused while reading his letter, and I pondered our different brains. I thought about the first time we'd met, at a conference, when he'd plopped down next to me at the round dinner table where I was sitting and announced quietly, intensely into the air, into me, "*Money ruins everything.*" I scanned his face and saw his soft heart on his chin, in its needy raisiny pucker. I noted the frustration in his concentrated, furrowed brow, as if he was trying to solve the unsolvable.

"Oh," I thought, "this is someone who isn't greedy. Who wants a real conversation."

I assumed autism from the length of his gaze, just a bit longer than intuition would have mandated. He later confirmed it for me, and it made sense to me that his brain was neurodivergent. Maybe that was why we saw each other clearly. The straightforwardness of him was calming to me, and his brain was talented in interesting ways.

I would come to consider him a friend and a good man. We began to write to each other, as it was a good way for us to ponder and converse.

I don't remember how I answered him when he wrote about big things being easier than little things. But in my head my answer is, "I always thought the little things were the big things. But you helped me through my divorce, and that's a big thing for me. The listening and the perspective. The willingness to tell me how you experienced yours." And when I was struggling with my writing, you said, "Write the truth. *The truth is always the most interesting.*"

So yes, the big things are big things. And they matter too.

Someone to Ask

"So I wanted to ask you because I need to ask someone ..." I paused.

"Go ahead," he encouraged.

"Well, when I was married and would get sad and frustrated, I thought, 'Who would ever want me? Three kids and middle-aged, who would want me now?' And then, when I finally started telling people that I was getting divorced ... Well, there was one offer after another. Some from men I'd known half my life or more—who asked straight out if they could take his place. All versions of 'I could ... I would ... love you better than he did.' None of it flowery, or showy, or insinuating. Every time, just straight and clear. And I need someone to ask, so I'm asking you ... *why?*"

"Ah, I see. Alright." His words slowed and warmed, settling deep in his throat. He sighed, "It's because you make us feel the connection we expected to find in marriage with our person ... but then didn't ... Many of us got married, and it's just not there, that connection we expected to have ... So, some of us got divorced, and some just settled into loneliness. And, well, some of us, like me, got divorced and re- ... Well, you know ... But you make it feel like that's still a possibility, that connection. That joy is still a possibility. You're wise and playful—that's an intoxicating thing for any man."

"I um ... Thank you."

"Yeah. No problem, Lovely. I'll call you tomorrow."

• • •

When I re-read this book for editing, I realized that much of this writing has to do with reclaiming my identity post-divorce. I've also been thinking lately about how the media right now seems to portray men— as a group—as unfeeling, disloyal, and cruel.

Make no mistake, there is evil in the world, and indeed, too many people have gotten away with too much for too long.

But also, in my life, in my experience, the men who have shown up for me are good and kind, supportive and steadfast. Not shallow or greedy or selfish.

So there's that.

My work is based on getting the assessment right—and that means also seeing good intentions where they are. Good humans are all around us.

Thank God.

In Love and in War

"You're like me."

"What do you mean?"

"My people have a saying. They say I'm 'first pick in Love and War.' That's you too. Everyone's first pick. In Love and in War."

"Oh. Yes. But I don't fight over the small stuff. And I don't go into battle for myself."

"Yeah, same."

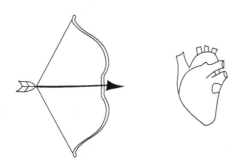

Intentions and Trust

"I'm not sure I'm saying this right. Let me try again," he said.

"You know, you don't have to say things right with me." I tucked one lip corner into my lifted cheek. My knowing smile. "I know what you mean, and I always know your intentions. We have so many years. You can say half a sentence, and I get it. Or if I don't, I'll ask. But I always know you mean well. You always do with me."

I puckered my chin, in vulnerability and in deep affection, just as he puckered his.

Mirroring.
Aligned.
Same.

• • •

Mirroring each other's body positions and facial expressions is how we connect in person. When I can't see someone's face, I find I make fewer facial expressions that match the emotions the other person expresses. So a conversation with a friend who is sad and hurting is easier and less emotional for me over the phone. If we are face to face, I mirror almost every expression and end up feeling like I've experienced all their emotions myself. That said, for those same reasons, I'm better able to soothe and offer comfort in person.

It should also be said that being able to touch and hug someone makes a huge difference in connection.

Dominos

S he said,
"I don't let
anyone in close,
not like this

close like you already are
close like you've always been,
only you and her

I can't make that space
anymore in my life,
in my broken,
wounded heart

so maybe love
it's not found between me and a man,
but real, life-long, healing love,
the profound kind,
is found in old friends
who know every bit of your soul
that you couldn't bear to show
anyone else
but since you're already here:
come in!
come in!
come in, I've missed you so"

like Dominos
three strong women,
three divorces,
three brave souls standing, finally
to say, "this does NOT work for me"

three prodigal daughters return

I can only imagine that our true matriarchs are smiling down
upon us
on this Reunion,
this Resistance,
this Resilience
the rhythm of your soft breathing
from the bed beside mine, imprinted on me

my safe space,
my forever home,
in the wooden cabins,
beneath the pine trees

"those of us," she said,
"who didn't have families
that kept us safe,
we have each other," she said

so let your tears flow freely
I've seen them before
and leave it to me
to remind you
who you are
because I know you like the back of my hand,
like a piece of my soul
and indeed
you know me,
as well

like Dominos
we fall
and like Dominos
we push each other
up again

(God bless Brown Ledge Camp)

• • •

In my life, it hasn't been the expected people who've taken best care of me. I don't think I ever felt entirely loved until fairly late in my life. Ironically by some of my oldest and dearest friends with whom I reconnected. I cannot put into words how utterly grateful I am. The relief of it changes every single thing.

DIARY OF A HUMAN LIE DETECTOR

Breathing Next to You

"I can breathe when I'm next to you," I sighed out the words.

"Well, that's good."

"No, I mean it. It's like I'm holding my breath everywhere, and I don't notice until you're next to me, and I lean into you, and, all of a sudden, I can breathe."

"Oh. Yeah, I get that. My son, next to me on the sofa. I can't stay awake. He puts me to sleep immediately. I worry about him constantly. But if he's next to me, I know he's safe. And then the exhaustion immediately overcomes me."

· · ·

There's a picture in the Glossary under **relief**.[64] It's me at a Starbucks leaning on this friend. He knows all of my flaws and weaknesses and none of them faze him. The picture was snapped before I realized it, and it captures me mid-divorce, in an unusual moment of peace. The lines between my eyebrows are still furrowed from stress. My eyes are shut—closing out the world—which we often do to marinate fully in emotion. I'm leaning into him, and my cheeks are risen in happiness, my chin puckered in vulnerability. And the corners of my lips are pulled—at once up and down—as is common in this soft, affectionate, platonic "love smile." I am grateful for him, and also for his wife, whom I loved from the very first moment. The way they look at each other makes my heart sing and reminds me that so much is good in this world. Still.

---

64   See #25 in the Glossary.

Almost for Sure

He said,
"most likely, probably, almost for sure
I won't steal your writings, your poems, your dress
even though, it all fits perfectly
and describes me, my experience, exactly
this last verse could be my business card"

I giggled, "you mean your gentleman calling card?
and also, you're not entirely surprised
surely you recognized, as I did at first meeting

thing this, this thing
two humans
two people
this word that my friend says is all powerful
same

despite all that is different
same
as in sameness of the soul"
I sighed

in life it is such
a relief to find
a friend

Flawed and Extraordinary, Also

I know
that I am flawed
and extraordinary

"both can be true"
that's what she always
says to me
when things seem
to be contradictory
but really they
are not

this is one of the ways
she loves me
by leading me through sorrow
and through the dark woods

with a snuggle and a snack
pulling things apart
and helping me to put words
on my ouchie bits

and sometimes she says,

"Annie, it's rest hour,
rest beside me
like when we were little
in the wooden cabins"

and I do

and I say to her
"when you trip,
no matter what,
I'll love you through it"

and I do

I love her through
her things
time and time
again

some loves
are platonic
and last
forever

like ours
also

· · ·

This is written about my best friend. She's the person I talk to most. She loves me through the hard bits of life, and I do the same for her. Also.

DIARY OF A HUMAN LIE DETECTOR

Now That It's Out of Me

"I'm going
to run,
now that it's all out of me,
all of the trauma.
I'm going to run."

She laughed gently,
"Okay, that's okay.
you can run to me,
I'll catch you."

It's Different Now

She said,
"I've laughed
more in the last four months
with you
than I did in the final
ten years of my marriage.
That says something."

"Yes, yes it does," I said. "That I'm funny as shit."

She giggled, "True."

Blasphemy!

" **B** lasphemy!" I yelled to my daughter. As I tasted the bite of the cream puff she handed me.

"Why would you ever put sugar into whipped cream?"

"Moooom, that face! That's FULL on disgust."

"Why? *Why*, when you know how I love real, fresh whipped cream! The Swede in me doesn't like the sweet. It ruins it."

She dissolved into giggles. "How can you care so much about that? Seriously, your face!"

"Mmmmn—noooooo," I protested. "I was expecting the whipped cream. I wanted the whipped cream. And right now, mid-world-falling-apart, I needed the whipped cream."

· · ·

There's a photo in the Glossary that shows my full face of **disgust**[65] with a bit of anger between my eyebrows. I'm squeezing the skin around my nose so much that my upper lip is pulled up. And there are deep lines from just above the corners of my nostrils down to the edges of my mouth. It's the NO Face ... the no, no, no, NO Face.

Keep in mind that once you add another emotion on the same face, it changes the emotional sentence. So, if you have raised cheeks and nostril shadows, usually accompanied by squished wrinkles on the sides of the nose, that would likely be delight in the uncomfortable — the face I make, for example, when someone says something wickedly **funny and inappropriate.**[66]

---

65   See #19 in the Glossary.
66   See #8 in the Glossary.

Emotional Insurance

" D eath and divorce," I've always said. "These are your people," I told my daughters. "These are the people who will love you through death and divorce. Through the hard, messy pieces of life. They know you.

Because in these summer weeks of living together 24/7, you can't hide your true self. So you love each other in a way others have little access to. For your real, quirky, weird selves.

These strong women, these lifelong friends
they show up for each other.
Over and over,
in the most difficult of times.

Sometimes after not seeing each other for years, or even decades,
but I've seen them come
to check one of their own into rehab, to comfort one another
after the loss of a child,
or the death of a spouse,
weddings, births, sickness, despair,
and sometimes simply loneliness.

They will climb into your bed, into your space, thinking nothing of closing the distance between you,
rubbing your shoulders, braiding your hair.
Offering without judgment: laughter, compassion, and silliness.
Silliness, sometimes the greatest relief of all.

They will remind you of who you are
and, in turn, you will make them remember who they were before
life became quite so complicated.
Your fountain of youth, of self, of love,
these are your lifelong friends.

Listen to me child, I know whereof I speak."

(Thank you to Brown Ledge Camp)

• • •

A beautiful piece of **sadness**[67] is the tilting of the eyebrows. In the upper face facial expression, there's a quick upwards hop or twitch of the inner eyebrows seen right above the nose. I rarely make this face without also showing worry.

When worry is present, the eyebrows raise less, because worry furrows the brows downwards while sadness lifts them. So the eyebrows end up compromising in the middle—often creating uneven wrinkles on my face where one brow is slightly higher than the other.

Many of the women I'm close to, like me, need to talk to think. To fully process emotion and human relationships, I need to vocalize. I'm in no way speaking for all women, but certainly the people I'm drawn to tend to share this pattern of talking as a way of processing, not just emotion, but also thought in general.

It's my way of fiddling, pulling apart, reaching conclusions, and setting strategy. It seems to me that people who need to process out loud tend to be particularly adept at social and emotional intelligence. Certainly talking with a friend, loved one, or therapist strengthens these muscles.

Also, loving feedback is useful, and if you are lucky, you have friends that call you out on your shit and make you roar with laughter while doing it. It is, for me, the best way to proceed with life, and I'm so very grateful.

I do have a few male friends who fall into this category as well. I hold them close to my heart and hug them tightly and often.

For whatever reason, I've never been romantically attracted to a man who processes emotions in the same way I do. For me, romantic attachment seems to necessitate a differently wired brain. Or maybe the man I love is so imprinted on me that there simply isn't space for an alternative.

---

67   See #27 in the Glossary.

Italian Stallion

"Italian Stallion," you called yourself,
  laughing at your own joke,
as you leaned forward to kiss me on the cheek,
as was custom, in introduction,
in that country,
foreign to us both

you sent seventeen-year-old me, instantly,
into fits of giggles
such a relief, in all my pain
I knew, instantly,
that we would be friends
for a long time

and when I saw you last,
at least a decade after the time before,
I raked my eyes over your face
as I'm wont to do with my children
and the people I love,
to ensure my heart
that you are safe and whole

I always called you by your real name,
not the name you took just for "that place"
simply because they said
your real one was a woman's name
I called you by your name because it's beautiful and I wanted
your pure self to myself
and you were always real
to me
with me

kind and soft
sarcastic and funny,
always soothing to me
warm,
in this sometimes cold, prickly world

• • •

I've noticed that I "rake" my eyes over the faces of the people I desperately love upon seeing them again after a long time apart. With my children, I do it often. It irritates them.

"Why are you looking at me like *that*?"

"I can't help it. It's a thing, you know, after a woman gives birth, to rake her eyes over the baby to see that the baby is healthy and whole. And, in your face and in the movement of your facial muscles, I see every piece of your emotional state. In our original human language."

"Ugh, Moooooom, I'm FINE."

With my students, in teaching them to look at the face—rather than just in the eyes—I *always* remind them not to stare too long at the lips. That will eventually get you kissed. Simply because, whether we realize it or not, this is what humans do when they want to be kissed.

So, when reading facial expressions, don't linger too long on the mouth.

I've learned this the hard way.

To Entertain Me

To entertain me, he'd start with a reasonable premise—and the businessmen lunching with us would eat it up—sometimes even pulling out paper or napkins to take notes. Then one idea after another would become more elaborate and outrageous as his cheeks would begin to rise in mirth, and the corners of his lips would fleetingly pop *downwards*. The men furiously noting, drawing circles and lists, and arrows between the circles and lists. Until his words became so utterly ridiculous that I could take it no more and would burst out, "LIAR!! You're such a pants-on-fire liar!!"

Whereby, the whole table would freeze in silence. After two beats, he would throw his head back, bellow with laughter, grin from ear to ear, with cheeks squished all the way up to his lower eyelids and say, "I thought you were going to stop me waaaaay earlier—I made it FAR this time. Gentlemen, if you'll excuse me, I have a VIP to entertain. Annie? Ready?"

We rose, synchronized, from our seats, businessmen stunned.

"Get some good expressions, Annie?" He grinned at me with his cocky grin—cheeks again up to his lower eyelids, and chin thrust up and forward. A half-smile playing on his lips, causing a single dimple next to the corner of the tucked lip. Almost hidden beneath his beard.

"Incorrigible!" I said, matching his grin and shaking my head, delighted.

"For you? I aim to please."

"Good, because I'd love a coffee."

He laughed as he reached over my head to push open the door in front of me, and we poured ourselves out into the Swedish sunlight.

His lies are to entertain me, impress me, and play with me.
Swedes love to play.

. . .

My absolute favorite people are the friends I can play with. I love banter and silly humor and large reactions. This piece is about an old friend who sometimes mentors me professionally. Or, well ... he tells me to do something, and it then takes me a decade to do it. (But see B—I finally wrote the book!)

This piece also makes me think about one of my favorite American clients who lets me play with his brain without judgment. He patiently allows me to test even my most shocking theories on him and laughs if I pull back and giggle and joke. He doesn't mind when he realizes I've said something crazy for the sole purpose of eliciting a facial expression, so I can play with his face or get it to turn a different shade of red or purple. Sometimes when my theories are unpolished or just plain wrong, he pushes back and asks questions that make me pause and commit to reexamining my thinking. Either way, we both end up with new things to ponder. And I enjoy talking with a friend who won't put me into a category or box that I wouldn't fit into anyway.

These are the expressions in this piece:

> Chin thrusts forward in **pride**.[68]

> Cheeks rise in **joy**.[69]

> A half-smile is a **knowing smile**.[70]

> Throwing his head back in laughter is abandoned **delight**.

---

68   See #24 in the Glossary.
69   See #11 in the Glossary.
70   See #12 in the Glossary.

His Favorite Game

The favorite game of my friend with the huge brain was to give me a flute of champagne, knowing I so rarely drink, to lubricate and loosen my already-unfiltered mouth.

Then he would demand impatiently that I read the room out loud, instead of only in my head, powerful man by powerful man, so he'd know who to invest in.

Also, he liked to laugh. As the alcohol infiltrated my blood, I would get more animated and exaggerated, knowing he still understood the gist. Knowing that he would keep me safe no matter what. This was an instant, visceral feeling the first time we met. That he was a protector. Who would protect *me*.

He did, many a time.

So my guard would drop, my armor would fall. And in went the drink.

I would show off for him in content and word play, switching from English, to Swedish, to French, and then to Spanish. Then ultimately to a smattering of freestanding German words, most of them wrong, and all of them out of context, because as it turns out, I don't actually speak German.

Finally, we would settle back into our almost-native Swedish, as it is most private, for drunken political strategies.

I would get him to giggle, and thereafter to belly laugh so loudly the room would pause in movement and noise. My cheeks risen in mirth, my chin protruded and thrust forward and up. In pride. Thrilled at his delight and gentle affection for my brain and ability to meet him at his level of wit and play. I knew this was rare for him.

At the end of the night
he would bear-hug me tight,
and I would sigh
and later sleep well,
sated from the laughter,
the snuggle and the unfiltered friendship.

Which really is the best kind.

...

Pride[71] has the forward-and-up movement of the jaw and often tips the head back a bit. It's always interesting to me to see it in context—to notice which other facial expressions accompany it. In this case, I show **affection**[72] in the lift of my cheeks with my closed mouth. **Mirth**[73] shows in a *slight* downturn of one or both of my lip corners (I would define this as "sass"—my eldest does this expression often). Sometimes there is also an added *tricksy* element shown by wrinkling and squishing the nose (wrinkles on the middle part of the nose on both sides).

Mirth tends to be a longer expression, and my daughter holds her mirth for at least a second.

This man often shows the **maybe**[74] expression with me when I say something surprising. The maybe expression also signifies, "Hmm, I'll have to think about that, I'm not convinced." Like mirth, the "maybe" is a downward pull of lip corners—but it is a hard, firm pull, and uses both lip corners simultaneously. It's a longer expression, possibly because it takes a bit of effort. I've also seen this expression show, "Wow, seriously, I'm impressed! Not bad, not bad."

---

71   See #24 in the Glossary.
72   See #14 in the Glossary.
73   See #18 in the Glossary.
74   See #17 in the Glossary.

Instigating

" I 'm not saying that. I'm just saying I won't instigate," I stated firmly.

She paused. Stopped in the street. Threw her head back as her words lifted straight out of her, "You've never not instigated in your life! You wake up in the morning and instigate! You open your eyes, and you're already instigating!"

"This. Time. I. Won't. Instigate."

She bent over. Laughter peeling out of her. Arms clutched around her midriff, as if holding in her sides would make the laughter skip the trajectory up and out of her. As we started dancing in the street. Mirroring each other's dance moves to non-existent music. First the mouse: dig-dig-dig into the air, then the sprinkler: spray-spray-spray. In front of the suburban houses.

A woman walking behind us, catching up. Her cheeks high up to her eyes as she grinned at us. Not even trying to stop her own laughter from escaping.

She wishes she was laughing and dancing in the street.

She wishes she was instigating.

Matzah Ball Soup

" **M** y meeting was canceled. So, I can come early. If ... if that works for you."

The answer came instantly. Her voice firm and warm.

"I'm in my PJs, the kids are home, it's Yom Kippur, and we're breaking the fast. Are you hungry? I'm making Matzah Ball soup. Come over. Can't promise I'll get dressed. Might. Might not. *Come.*"

"I feel like every person I ever call should answer just like that," I said. *Just like that.* Warm and open, making space.

My chin puckering. Vulnerable. My cheeks rising. Safe and happy. I've so missed this. Missed you.

• • •

The expressions in this piece:

> The chin puckers in **vulnerability**.[75]

> The cheeks rise in **joy**,[76] pushing out smile bags under the eyes.

---

75   See #29 in the Glossary.
76   See #11 in the Glossary.

You Feel Like Home

"You know," I said to him with my body curled up on his sofa, my shoeless feet tucked in between two cushions. He had just made me laugh the way he did when we were children. That belly laugh where you throw your head back, and it bursts out of you. My eyelids softened, slipping part of the way down my irises, not in flirtation, but in acquiescence, relief, and emotional surrender. I reached one hand down to scratch the warm, brown dog curled up next to me on the sofa. "You make every single thing in this world better. *Every. Single. Thing.* Is better because you are here." I held my gaze on him to let the words sink in along with my eternal gratitude to this friend, who'd steered me safely through my teenage years.

"Thank you. I don't feel that way. But thank you."

"It's true. And I know you don't. But it's true, nonetheless. Every. Single. Thing."

"You," he said softly. "You feel like home. I feel like I'm home now that you're here. I haven't felt that way in a really long time."

I knew what he meant. He had been family to me at a time when we shared an unspoken understanding that neither of us quite *fit*. I wondered if he needed me here for a moment to finally, fully surrender to the idea of moving back to the place where we grew up. To remember a few more of the good pieces, for there were those too. Every time I visited him, his wife, and their son, I would sigh, happy that they always acted like they had been waiting impatiently. This family who loved me enough not to run the vacuum before I came. They believed me when I said, "We're not the kind of friends who need to tidy up before a visit."

He Drew Me a Cat

"I was numb, but now I'm raw."

"I'm so sorry," he said. "I can't do much over text. I have meetings, and then I have to go home. This is news to me. How long has it been bad?"

"A while. A long time."

"I can't do much from here. Do you want me to draw you a cat?"

"Yes, please. A cat would be good."

"You know, I'm a dog person."

"Me too."

"But I'll draw you a cat. I can do that. And I'll see you soon. Text me when you land."

• • •

"He's going to draw me a cat. Jesus, this man gets me on a cellular level." I told our mutual friend on the phone later that day.

"Yes, he's good like that."

"He knows I wind upwards, and even through his texts I can hear his soft, steady voice reminding me that he's solid and still, and I can hold on tight. He doesn't mind if I lean into him and breathe. Even when the waves make me nauseous."

I tilted my head in vulnerability, pulled in and up on the muscles in my chin, and puckered my lips tightly. Squeezed my eyes to release the tears. Even talking about him lowered my defenses, made me safe enough to actually feel all of my emotions. *Finally.*

"Yes, he's good like that," she said. "He's always been good like that."

. . .

This is a cat. From the 80s.
From a letter that he sent me from his summer camp.
He still offers to draw me cats.
Because, well, drawing dogs is hard.

The Man from the Mob

The man from the mob was really just a little boy who wanted to hang out and giggle.

My friend and I would entertain him, this sorrowful, regretting person, at town meetings. My friend and I were already in the habit of saying and doing ridiculous things to take the edge off of life in suburbia. Instead of grown women, we more closely resembled two fourth-grade boys, showing off and double-dog-daring each other to say inappropriate things. The usually-despondent man enjoyed every minute of it.

So, when he came to his last town meeting, my friend and I naughtily suppressed giggles all the way through the pontificating, presenting people. The man scurried over to us after the listening portion of the evening was done, pouted with his lips, and said glumly, "I kept trying to make my way over to you two who were having all the fun in the room. And to get to you, I would have had to climb over the laps of several boring men. They probably wouldn't have appreciated that ..."

My friend piped up and offered generously, "We had a meeting last week at the boring board we're on together. It was at the board president's house.

"The entire house was decorated with roosters: towels, paintings, salt and pepper shakers, potholders, candles, vases, knickknacks of every kind. Well, every 'rooster' kind, anyway. Roosters, roosters everywhere. And Annie, when she shook the homeowner's hand, she said, without cracking a smile, 'You must *really* like cock.' And then walked away, leaving me cryyyyyyying! I couldn't get a word out when I was supposed to be shaking his hand!"

The man bellowed and grinned, his cheeks rising high on his face. "I knew I was seated in the wrong section. Keep talking, ladies. You have no idea how long it's been since I've really laughed."

We did. We knew at that point how out-of-control his life had gotten. So we gifted him with unfiltered laughter for the rest of the evening, to soothe his weary soul.

As he awaited his sentence to atone for his sins.

Boys Who Get on Planes

"I'm getting divorced," I told him.

"Oh *good*. And by the way. What is your speaking tour schedule? I could meet you in London. It's an easy trip for me." Smooth, soft voice. Pause. "I could come, Annie."

My silence.

Him, gently, "I mean, I could just come for the day. Show you the city, in a way you haven't seen it before. I can be there early in the morning. Everything will be okay. It will be alright." Swift switch to speak in Swedish, melodic and calming. The rhythm of it reaching deep into my marrow. *Safety.*

"Everyone else is shocked," I plead. "They are all questioning me. Not you. You act like you think I know what I'm doing. It helps. So much. Not to be underestimated."

"Well, I know you, and I assume you've come to this conclusion after much thought."

"Yes!"

"Well then. London? I could come Sunday?"

Tears swelling in my eyes, throat thick and vocal cords tight, constricted. This boy, this man, who didn't even need to be asked.

My right hand moving to grasp my neck, palm covering my vulnerable suprasternal notch, the deep dimple in the center of my collar bone. My fingers curling, rubbing, and soothing the skin on my neck then stretching out to rise, to reach up my neck. Then sliding down again and curling inwards. Slowing my breathing, my heart rate, soothing my achy soul.

• • •

When humans feel **vulnerable**,[77] we often cover our lower necks. I do this all the time myself when I feel uncomfortable or unsafe. It's one of my favorite things to play with when I give workshops—if I say things that are slightly inappropriate I can get almost every person in the audience to cover their necks ... then I explain what I just did.

---

77   See #30 in the Glossary.

Accommodating

He slows way down when he doesn't follow what you mean,
and you should pause and let him think,
or he'll get frustrated
this is because he's filtering and doesn't want to multitask
he needs to process, to think in solitude

let him, without interrupting
he'll be easier to get along with,
and so much less crabby

by the way,
if you haven't bantered with him fast and loose,
you haven't lived
you win, he giggles
he wins, he giggles

so, either way
you win

Do Me!

"Ok, do me! What was I thinking the first time we met?"

"That I was hot."

"*Totally!*"

. . .

Mirth[78] is a smug-*ish* and happy expression that has pieces of affection and joy in the risen cheeks, as well as playfulness shown in the lip corners that are at once lifted and pulled down. Sometimes mirth will have a slight chin lift of pride as well, as in, "See, I got you!"

We humans mirror both facial expressions and body language when we are emotionally connected or aligned. When "me" becomes "we." And for those of us who recognize it in the moment, there is an additional layer of intimacy.

With some people, I know, instantly, at the first meeting, that we fit. That we "get" each other and that we will be close and supportive of each other for a long time. Human attachment based on deep friendship is a beautiful thing indeed. I no longer question the instinct that standing in front of me is one of my people. I relax and surrender to it. They catch up eventually to the same realization, sometimes a long time later.

But catch up they do.

Lucky me.

---

78   See #18 in the Glossary.

Longing & Loss

The World is Ruled by Broken-hearted Men

King Edgar
of the winter freeze,
was once a different man
before despair and isolation,
and he declared, "I AM!"

King Edgar of the ice age,
of the nothing-matters stage,
of the I'm alllllll work, and
"I don't really care if anyone sits next to me ...
but *maybe* ... maybe you can rule beside me,
as long as you don't kick me off the throne,
and seduce all my disciples
with warmth and wit,
with kindness and tender words

as long as you never leave me again"

the world is ruled
by broken-hearted men
all hail!
and bow
to the King
of broken hearts

for he will
TAKE all the love that he was once denied

when love remains elusive,
power becomes
the only way
to rule the chaos that resides,
inside the soul
of the boy King

and I would tell you,
if I thought you were open to listening,

**that lack of empathy
facilitates the rise to power**

but, alas, indeed,
(and totally for sure)
it also *ensures*
its downfall

• • •

I'll say it again: lack of empathy facilitates the rise to power and also ensures its downfall. Men who are numb to the reactions of others often rise more easily to power.

However, when they get there, they often have a hard time maintaining their power. This is because they've established very little loyalty, protection, or friends who are willing to keep them clued in to the happenings and charged emotions around them. And these men are now bigger take-down targets than ever.

One of my friends was lamenting recently how many bad decisions were made in the company he works for—as if the decisions were poorly thought-out and strategized.

It seemed to me that these bad decisions were short-term strategies to mostly benefit the person making them. "That's what's the problem," as my son used to say when he was little. The problem is that when selfish, power-hungry people are promoted, they rarely make good long-term decisions for the business, if they have the choice to make shorter-term solutions that benefit themselves individually more. They usually choose strategies that seem plausible enough, defendable enough, so they don't get into too much trouble. Detached, numb humans are rarely good at making choices for others.

Must be tremendously lonely

so

very

lonely

I've been lucky enough to work with some great leaders who truly have purpose. That changes every single thing for the organizations and for the people attached to them in both their personal and professional lives. It certainly gives my work meaning, allows me to share my gifts wisely, and helps me to make an impact where it matters. I'm so very grateful to be in a position where I can choose who I work with, both when it comes to individuals and organizations.

Gauntlet

I ran the gauntlet
  sailed the sea
showed you every piece of me
I moved the mountain
wrote the book

did all that I could do for you
now let me go
now let me be
release me,
from this destiny
recuse me,
for all eternity,
this time,
this final time

let

  me

    go

You pushed the paper with my writing back to me. "That's a little ... mean."

I lifted my chin and let out one piece of laughter, more relaxed than I usually am with you, "Yeah, it kind of is. I'm okay with that."

• • •

The chin lifts in both **pride**[79] and defiance. In this case, momentarily at least, I was proud to be defiant.

Ugh for pride, which in our case, has often gotten in the way of love.

---

79   See #24 in the Glossary.

And led,
over and over
to loss

my loss
his loss
our loss

. . .

(I miss you.)

Maybe

Maybe you sabotaged us
on purpose
because it was too big,
bold, brave, and real

how terrifying that there are
bits of your soul
that only I can reach

your anxiety has become so well-versed
that you find a strange comfort
in the pain

as you wander
by my childhood home,
walk your dogs and
marinate in the ache

you may live on it,
but it will always be
my Street

and oh sweet Lord
back to where
we started

as I miss you:

*I'll take a beat
and wait here
breathing
slow and deep*

Wired and Wound

We met when I was upside down,
 wired and wound,
and stuck in a past
with no future
pulling myself out of my pain by my fingertips
wobbly

and yet
your gaze was clear,
needy,
lonely,
begging with your eyes

saying:
see me, please, because
my soul has been misunderstood,
denied
betrayed
for so long

oh!

um ...

unexpected

• • •

A **sad**[80] expression makes the eyebrows pull up in the middle of
the forehead to form a triangle. The skin underneath the eyebrows
collapses and often makes a diagonal line from the outside corners of
the eyes, up toward the top of the nose bridge. The chin pushes in and
up, causing a prune-ish, raisin-ish look and forcing the middle section

---

80   See #27 in the Glossary.

of the bottom lip to jut out. This protruding bottom lip is how I'm able to see if a man with a beard is showing sadness or vulnerability.

Vulnerability[81] is a piece of sadness—so I can't always see exactly whether a person is just feeling vulnerable or sad from the chin alone. Vulnerability without sadness wouldn't have the diagonal skin on the eyelids, though. And really, context usually gives me the other clues I need. Also, I ask questions or say more things to dig a little deeper— and in the repetition of the expression, I find my proof.

In **anguish** and **devastation**,[82] the bottom lip forms a rectangular shape. I see that as a piece of fear, which makes sense because when we are really in pain—emotional or physical—we fear it won't go away. Pain is frightening in part because it feels permanent.

---

81 See #29 in the Glossary.
82 See #23 in the Glossary.

About Myself, He Said

"I don't like
talking about myself," he said
as he pursed his lips into a slight pout.

"You love me." I said, right *into him.*

"Yes." He nodded instantly, firmly, then grabbed my eyes in his. The speed at which he answered proving that it was deep in him, this truth between us. The truth spills fast, before the brain is able to catch up.

"And even with me," I continued, "it takes time for you to melt. Twenty minutes or so. To remember to surrender. *And it's me.* I get it, because I panic when I see you too. It's always more feeling, more everything, than my body is prepared for. It's different with us. So I understand that you are wound. But you have to figure out how to let people in. You have to *sometimes* let some people in."

"I don't like talking about myself," he repeated obstinately, with a break in his voice.

"Yes, but you need to connect with your wife.
This woman you chose.
Maybe *she* needs it.
And then it would be the generous thing, the kind thing.
It's what we do for the people we love, we compromise.
It's not only about what suits you.
Maybe she needs you to share yourself and your thoughts.
To feel close to you. To feel happy and safe. Connected.
You have to find a way to be good at intimacy.
It's not fair to her otherwise
for you to stay in a marriage that you don't participate in."

"I'm not. Good at it. Intimacy, *I'm not.*"

"Yes, yes you are," I said, holding his gaze to prove my point. "We've always had it, our entire lives. If you can do it with me, then you can do it. You have to learn to trust. I know that's partly my fault. That I broke it when we were young."

He nodded bitterly, with a puckered chin and a quick rectangularing of his bottom lip. Agony.

"Yes, you did," he agreed. Letting me pull the blame onto myself. I hoped that it provided him some relief, my participation in his sorrow. This stubborn, prideful man whose coldness stemmed entirely from his scarred and broken heart.

"Find a way," I pleaded,
"To be happy
in the life
that you chose.
Love her the way you would have loved me."

"I can't. Not that much." He tried to muster a laugh at his own "joke." Meaning the words as a compliment. A sorrowful, lonely compliment.

The intensity of the exchange was causing pain in my solar plexus, and I turned my gaze out to the horizon. Willing myself to look elsewhere for solace and calm. I nodded once, feeling my chin pucker and my lower lip protrude in grief.

I wanted to climb into bed in a dark room, cocoon myself under heavy covers. Let the feeling of sorrow swallow me until it washed all the way through me, only releasing its hold when numbness and hunger overwhelmed it. At this age, I was familiar with loss. Knew that surrender was the only way through it to the other side. I had made a conscious commitment to myself to allow my feelings free range of my body. That, ironically, seemed to be the only way to deny them permanent infiltration. To stop pain from building a nest inside me.

"Try. Figure it out," I pleaded. "*Try*. I need only one thing from you. I need you to stay alive. That's it. This level of stress for such a long time causes heart attacks in men our age. Stay. On this planet. Do you understand?"

His chin mirrored mine. Dimpling, puckering, pained. Tears swelling in his eyes and mine.

"Try." I nodded again, pushing my knee against his, nudging him to agree with me.

He mirrored my nod, short and tight. Seemingly acquiescing.

And I realized that he was lying to me. He knew he wouldn't try. Somehow, for some reason, when I was sleeping across the ocean, he had decided that he didn't deserve happiness. That work and only work, would be his full, permanent endeavor.

My heart whispered to his: "I would forgive you all of your flaws, all of your sins. Even if I knew them all, I would still love you. I have no illusions of perfect humans. No need or want of them. But *this*. This visceral thing between us, defying rhyme and reason and time. Defying us both ..."

And I remembered the tightness in his voice when I told him of my imminent divorce, and he turned away from me, tucked his chin to his chest, slumped his shoulders, and lamented, "Not everyone gets to marry the right person."

• • •

The lip corners pulling down and out toward each respective shoulder show me his **devastation** and **anguish**.[83] They "flash" quickly as he

---

83   See #23 in the Glossary.

tries to control his pain. This is what I call rectangularing the lower lip. God, at this point in our lives, I've seen this expression on his face many times. I've caused it many times.

Most days, I am endlessly grateful for my abilities, the decades of work I've put into my obsession with reading others. But other days, it hurts to see struggle and pain, raw and unveiled, undeniable, and right in front of my face. Especially in the faces of my loves. His face in particular.

Also, how devastatingly sad for this martyred man who continues to lament that he wishes he'd married me.

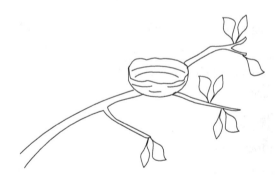

Lost in the Woods

D ivorce is
like getting lost
in the woods at night
with no way to find your way back home
you need someone to call
and say,
"can you please come get me?"

(Thank you, EFJ, for coming to get me.)

The Window

" I 'm sorry I missed the window," he said.
"I got stuck at the office"

me too
I'm sorry you missed it too
I so rarely leave the window open these days,
when the air outside is so raw and frigid
and my heart, so fragile

it's closed now,
in case you were wondering
so, you're safe
and I'm safe

but not really

I Think

I think
I scare the crap out of you
when I'm the one who should be scared
really, this is adult love?
this is dumb

My Good Poems

One should
not drink
if one writes poetry

or said poetry
could be sent poetry

or worse, said to the person
who doesn't,
shouldn't,
might not
deserve
to hear it

Oops.

Never Had That

" I 've never ... had that,"
he said to me when
my breathless words were finished,
"I've wanted it, looked for it,
but never found it

so, I'm thrilled and anxious,
terrified and so very turned on
after you spoke of your desires out loud
to me
I'm touched. In more ways than one ..."

"Come," I said to him,
"I'll be so very tender with your body and soul,
but please,
be gentle with my fragile heart"

About Me

" **S**o, I've written three books now and every single one of them is going to get me in trouble."

"Are they ... I mean how much do I ... feature?"

"You mean are they all about you?"

"Yes, are they?"

"You feature. *Always*, but they are more about someone else."

Silence. Slump. "Oh. Do I want to know?"

"The main character is me. I guess it always was."

He quieted, held my gaze. "Yeah, that's fair. Probably about time."

"Yeah." I grinned at him, "Seriously, could you even be any needier?"

"Only for you. *Only. For. You.*" He smiled sadly at me, his cheeks risen, his chin puckered, and the skin between his inner eyebrows lowering in a diagonal line out to the outer edges of each eyelid.

Sadness. Loss.
I see it my Love,
I do.

• • •

Oh, for love and longing. He does the expression of longing better than anyone I've known in my lifetime. I've never quite managed to find a perfect photo of this expression. But oh, for his raisiny chin and needy, slopey eyebrows that hit me right in my solar plexus every time.

Lies & Betrayal

Epiphany

I t also occurs
to me
that a healthy relationship probably
doesn't require a shit-ton of therapy
this should probably not be an epiphany

oh well

The Rebound

S ometimes someone shows up for a very short
time in life
and shows you what it's like to feel
and laugh and live

and it turns out
ultimately
that he isn't who I needed or wanted him to be
but the reminder of *who I am*
and how I'm capable of feeling and giving and loving

is so very welcome indeed

All You Can Ask

All you can ask of someone
is that they show you who they are
you did
and I'm done
and still waiting for the relief
to come and chase away *the hurt*

How About This

An arrogant, entitled man once asked me
for advice on how to improve his relationships

how about this:
don't be an entitled douche

(And also, maybe don't ask if you're not really interested in my answer
and only using your questions to get close to me in a creepy way.)

It's in the Way You Lie

When you lied and pretended you didn't, because a technicality in your sentence made it true, but your intention was to mislead me and seduce me under false pretenses,

that's almost dirtier than if you just straight-up lied, because you did it this way to claim smugness, superiority, and intellectual craftiness at the expense of my heart, and it showed me I don't matter to you at all.

That's not how I felt about you.

• • •

Most humans try not to lie, so they insert qualifiers into a sentence to make it true when it *wouldn't* be true without the qualifier. Note, I don't say "all humans," because that would be a lie.

I feel compelled to clarify that none of the poems about deception and betrayal are about the man to whom I write most of the loving poems.

He only ever wanted to love me, despite all of our fears and all of our flaws.

Qualifiers and a Mostly Good Guy

" I 'm *mostly* a good guy."
Bahahaha, that was a qualifier for SURE.
Why are you not a good guy?

"I *tend* to honor my commitments."
Weirdest response ever to, "Are you going to stay married?"

"Are your windows closed?"
"Yeah they *should* be."
"That was a qualifier—go check your windows."

"Emma, did you eat a cookie?
(four-year-old Emma with a face full of chocolate crumbs)
"No Mama, I did not eat *a* cookie."
"Emma, did you have *two or more* cookies?"
"Yeaaaaah."

"My feelings for you are *mostly* platonic."
Ummm ...? So your romantic feelings?
How's that going?

"How much sleep did you get last night, Love?"
"I *might* have gotten a couple hours, Mom."
"Or maybe you didn't sleep?"
"Yeah, not really ..."

Funny how qualifiers are funny.

My Talk

"So I'm launching a new talk, or series, maybe it's a series, but either way..."

"Really? On what? I like your talks, can I come? Or are you filming it?"

"I'm not sure you would want to."

* * *

Later ... I added in my head, what I would have liked to have said to him ... "The workshop is called *Facial Expressions in Love and Arousal: How to know if someone's really into you or only wants you for sex*. It's years of research. You wouldn't like it because the verbal examples of lying, they are from you, from the very short time we knew each other. You gave the best examples.

And the piece that's really interesting is that I also knew it at the time, my brain raising flag after flag. Each stained in red. And I know about your trauma, the awful things you endured. I know. I guess I would be angrier if I didn't. But it's hard to be furious at a man who is never going to figure out how to love and be loved. Who has in him potential that will most likely never be realized.

Unless you decide to become a better man and do the actual work to get there ... I won't hold my breath, though. My friend, the new one that I'm so attached to, I love him in part because he's figuring a way out. He's finding his way through the tunnel of darkness to end the cycle of abuse, so he can protect others. If that's not magnificent, I don't know what is."

Silence.
Silence.
More silence.

Dirty Secrets

I never promised to keep your dirty secrets
you just assumed that I would be ashamed

why should I be afraid?
the people who love me know me
trust me
rely on me
and rightly so
they know I am solid and true

unlike you

the older I get, the less ashamed I am
for the bad things that were done to me

your house of cards is a puff of wind away
from falling down

what's that I hear?
no matter
it's only the wind
gently blowing
from my mouth

• • •

One of the bravest, truest things I've ever seen is my friend Dave, in his 50s, witnessing to our old school board in Glencoe, Illinois about how he was sexually assaulted as a child by one of the district's teachers. Dave stood up and spoke of the assault and said, "I'm not ashamed, because I was a child when it happened." I watched the faces of the school board and the superintendent and saw their jaws drop open in shock at his clarity.

He was utterly magnificent.

That's not exactly what happened to me, but still it was bad enough that, even now, I'm working on putting it into words.

Silence isn't an option.

Thank God that powerless children so often grow into powerful adults.

And thank you to Dave Stroud, and our friend John Bollman[84] as well, for modeling the courage to stand up to pedophiles, as well as to the bullies who protect them.

And to the wolves in sheep's clothing, that still "stand guard" over Glencoe, our childhood home:

May your sleep ever be interrupted
by the ghosting cries of the children
you've betrayed.

---

84   John Bollman is a survivor of pedophile Charles Ritz who taught in Lake Bluff, Illinois. John has made it his life's mission to fight for justice for survivors of sexual assault and help ensure that other kids don't have to experience what he did. John helped us in the investigation of Glencoe, Illinois teacher and pedophile Marvin Martin. Marvin Martin was my 6th-grade teacher, and one of my classmates told me that he had been molested by Martin a couple years after it happened. I did sound the alarm but was ignored. Only Dave Stroud—whom I found/met online in 2017 when my guilt of not having done more got the better of me—was willing to go public. To be clear, Dave is not the classmate who told me he had been molested by Martin in 6th grade. So now there were two victims that had told me about Martin, neither of whom knew each other. In 2017, three grown Glencoe kids: Dave Stroud, Kate Elisco, and I, formed an investigative team together with John Bollman. With the help of our Glencoe network, we eventually found a total of eight victims. We believe there were hundreds. Several survivors seemed to reason that because we were past Illinois' statute of limitations, it wasn't worth the trauma of going public. One other survivor witnessed anonymously, but his statements appear to have "disappeared." We're periodically still in touch with that survivor, and my belief is that he and others will someday speak openly. The Glencoe School District has still not acknowledged that Martin was a pedophile. A huge thank you to Chuck Goudie and Barb Markoff of ABC7 Chicago for helping Dave tell his story. It meant everything to us (https://abc7chicago.com/marvin-martin-glencoe-sex-abuse-teacher/2389082/). A huge thank you also to all the other individuals who publicly and privately helped us with the investigation, especially Lesley Barton. It matters.

Behold the Alliance

S ometimes
very quietly
in the dead of night
over wine and popcorn
an alliance is formed

not in anger
but in realization that it is time for the cycle of abuse
to come to an end
it ends with us

our weapons of choice:
kindness and mischief

who imagined?
that we would rise and lift each other up
and that one plus one
is so very much more than two

when we are together, you hold no power,
strength, or sting over us
and indeed if you snap and snarl and bite
we will laugh it off, as we collude

you understand that
we do fully beat you
we so fully win your stupid game
when we love and support each other
so you have naught the tools to
tear us down

raise a glass, sister of mine
and I will raise mine too
kindness and mischief and mirth
so their bitter words won't pierce
through our thickened skin

Quick and Dirty

When I write about him,
it's because his fingerprints are on my soul

when I write about you,
it's quick and dirty,
to expunge you
like squeezing out a pimple,
so you won't infect me
or leave a stain

though I thought maybe you'd fill
a different void,*
a friend or perhaps a lover,
you had nae the kindness,
nor the character

and indeed,
a villain I did need,
you'll do just fine for that

you betrayer of women,
of men,
enemy of your own naked,
shattered heart

I believe you when you say
in your childhood home
there was no love,
because, really, could there be any other explanation?

be better,
do better
figure out how to love yourself,
so you can spread other than misery around you

there is something decent buried deep
underneath all your pain,
I am almost certain of it
if indeed you choose to water it,
give it sunlight and
let it grow

• • •

*Ugh yes, I can't even make it through a crabby poem without innuendo, it's an affliction, really.

Also, I should note that when I gave this poem to a fellow writer to read, he wrote back a *whole thing* about what you should and shouldn't do with and to pimples. Not the point, Dude.

But still ... kind of funny.

Lying to Myself

I t's annoying not to be
able to lie to myself
my leaky expressions
always tell me the real bits
of how I feel about that and this,
and of course how I feel about you and you
and him and her
and them and them,
as well
(jobbigt ibland)

• • •

At this point, I trust my face and its constant, never-ending connection to my subconscious to show me what to do and whom to trust. Such a strange surrender.

Toeing the Line

I toe
the line
of what is socially awkward,
slightly emotionally inappropriate ...

so that I can get good facial expressions,
a real read on whether you show contempt or kindness
when I clumsily step out of line

if you find relief in the fact that while
what I'm saying may not be entirely within your social rules,
I am, at the very least, authentic and insightful (I am)

the easiest way to see under all of your armor is to remove mine
so, I see instantly if real and funny pleases you,
and I can get a proper read on your baseline,
read the kindness or hostility in your naked expressions and

indeed also see if the room holds
any wolves
dressed
in wool

• • •

The clearest, simplest way for me to see if someone is lying is to watch
and see if their facial expressions are congruent with their words.
Happy words should go with a happy expression. Kind words should
go with a kind expression. Angry words should go with an angry
expression ... etc. Of course, life is hard and messy and complicated,
and oftentimes we try to present ourselves, our abilities, and our lives
as better than they really are. That's understandable, and it's okay to
be human and flawed.

The problem is when someone exhibits predatory behavior while saying sugary-sweet words to a child, for example. That would look like the sinister pieces of contempt, the **NO face**,[85] anger, etc., while saying something flattering.

Think of a growling wolf or snarling witch in a fairytale ... *that's a problem.*

---

85   See #19 in the Glossary.

The Needy Client

Y ou should
  have asked me to dance
when I was sitting
by myself

when I needed the work
the money
the connections
when I was new to this region

when over and over,
I worked my magic to teach
you the skills you needed
to negotiate with others

when I said I'm tapped out,
I need you to pay me
for the multitude I teach you:
this is, after all, my profession

later, later, later, you said
and you
delayed, delayed, delayed

and now?
now, when my dance card is full and
I am well loved
well friended
well connected
well paid
and well *known*

now you are surprised that I lift my lip and wrinkle my nose
at the crumbs and shackles
you offer me
so late in the day

I remember that you
greedily took all
that I offered
for free

can't control the market, you say?
what you can't control
is me

· · ·

When I talk to people about deep loyalty, they often bring up someone who was there for them in a time of crisis. Helping someone when they are especially needy for the help is remembered for a very long time. It often serves as the foundation of a solid, lasting relationship. But the opposite is true as well, not showing up to help or simply taking advantage of someone because you can ... well that's not often forgotten either.

This piece references the **NO Face**.[86] Other names I sometimes use for this expression include the:

> "EW" face

> "I don't want to" face

> "this icks me out" face

> "this makes me uncomfortable" face

> "this smells bad" face

---

86   See #19 in the Glossary.

There are three major pieces of this face:

1. The **lifting of the top lip**, all the way across, or only on one side (I often lift the left side of my top lip).

2. The **wrinkling on the sides of the nose**, as if one is trying to shorten and contract the length of the nose (say "Ewwwww!" and you almost have to do this).

3. The **nostril shadows**—the deep shadowing next to the nostrils. Sometimes this shadow line stretches all the way down from its curled hook above each outer nostril to the lip corner on the same side of the face.

My kids and I watch Jimmy Fallon, and my daughter Lea interned for him on *The Tonight Show*. He does an amazing series of skits where he pretends to be a teenage girl and says, "EW!" I tell my students to watch these clips to practice—it's perfect for learning both the NO Face and the face of **joy**[87]—since he so often breaks character and slips into his contagious giggles. This is obviously my favorite part. Watch how one expression transforms into the other and what they look like together.

If you look for only one thing in the NO Face, look for the nostril shadows—just like the smile bags show clear joy, the nostril shadows are proof of NO.

The **nostril shadows** mean: "No, something smells off!"

---

87   See #11 in the Glossary.

The Ally

I can't be your ally
and your adversary
or to put it bluntly
I won't

if I am to protect you
provide for you
promote you
and catapult you forward

then you must
be appreciative
of the pieces of me
that sacrifice
my own peace

the parts of your situational complexity
that spin my brain
and steal my sleep
so I can find solutions
hidden to all others

you must always treat me as an equal
at the very least
and in the way I tell you
you are to treat me
I'm clear in my communication
remember to hear me

and just because no one has ever been able to
get into your brain,
your work,
or your heart
like I do

you must still respect my boundaries
and understand that even though
I can see into your soul
that you cannot
and may not
see into mine

understand that to do otherwise
means you lose me

recognize me
fully
as your ally
and I will lift you,

but

I cannot negotiate *with* you
cannot go to war *against* you
if I'm your ally
or to put it simply
I won't

you'll simply awaken
one day
and I'll be gone

aligned with someone else
far, far away
who better knows
how to treat a
Queen

· · ·

Loyalty has always felt like survival to me, and I've tended to let go of relationships when I've come to understand that the other person doesn't value loyalty the way I do. I'm often surprised in business situations when I observe someone in power taking for granted someone whom they desperately need. This almost never works out, and the person in perceived power seems, to me, to have so much more to lose.

Also, it simply isn't kind, and kindness matters.

You Suck at Love

D ude,
  you suck at love
and I know you're broken
battered and bruised
and indeed I know why

but seriously, life is short
so be better,
be more for her

or get out,
set her free
and for God's sake, get help
so you can participate in raising
your own children
before it's too late

you have no right to reside in your beautiful family
if you only offer
anger, aloofness, and anxiety

if all you give your wife is money,
and never kindness
then surely you understand,
that you're treating the mother of your children
like a prostitute

(Prostitutes deserve kindness too.)

• • •

I wrote this about a man I knew for a short time, who tried to convince me that he was separated from his wife. He wasn't separated, or separating, or going to separate. Turns out this was his "usual game." Lucky me—the red flags flew bright and high before he could ever touch me. I was surprised though, by how much he hurt both my feelings and my pride.

Anger[88] has tight lips. The lips can be open and tight, closed and tight, or pushed out into a pucker and tight. The top part of the anger expression creates one or two vertical lines of stress between the eyebrows from the hard pull down and toward the middle of the nose. **Deep thinking**[89] creates the same furrowed lines between the eyebrows but lacks the tight lips. Whenever I see tight lips, I know there is a piece of anger in the expression. Even if there also exist other emotions and expressions in the person's face at the same time. We humans are both simple and complex, and we OFTEN feel multiple emotions simultaneously.

I'm also more and more aware as I grow older that sometimes men and women who are very broken develop an almost hyper-sexuality and are able to be super intense in their fleeting initial contacts—it's not real intimacy, but it does indeed feel like it.

Without this hyperintensity, how else would they be able to keep the interest of romantic partners despite their terrible behavior?

This intensity is also necessary in order to seduce new victims, because the old ones eventually catch on.

---

88   See #1 in the Glossary.
89   See #2 in the Glossary.

Recipe for Deception

He preps them, the women, by initially being brutally honest. Talking, even in groups of strangers, about the hard bits of his life, the flaws in his character. Sometimes, he whispers these confessions to a woman seated next to him, and follows it with a long and lingering look. *Do you see me? Is it okay that I have this flaw? Might you, possibly, want me anyway?*

He says, "I'm open and real in a way that none of my peers or colleagues are. Just me. Honesty matters to me. They all pretend and hide their true selves, but you can't really connect to people that way." He says, "Why pretend, when we all have a hard time? I show my flaws, it makes others feel comfortable and safe ..." (Indeed it does.)

By confessing "his things," he gets others to open up. Only they tell him with an open heart, relieved to find "true" connection. He listens well, maintains eye contact well, hugs warmly. Seemingly saying, "I see you, I see you, we are the same."

He, he is working. Working clients, working her. He laces all of his lies with the truth, always a kernel at the base, knowing they land best that way. His apparent earnestness comes from actually believing himself to be the victim.

He says his marriage is over, he has been too hurt, too frozen, too dead inside to do anything about it. Has utterly given up on connection ... his wife hates him, his parents never loved him, his anxiety and his loneliness are, at times, crippling. Sometimes he just exists, the numbness overtaking everything, but oh God, it feels so good to laugh *finally*! What a relief to laugh with a woman like her, to be truly seen by a woman like her! Sleep is elusive to him, he says. He looks her deep in the eyes as if to say ... if you were with me ... I would be safe and loved and whole, and sleep would come easily.

"I've never met anyone like you," he says. With longing and lust.

Much of his story, his theater, is based in reality, but it's all used as a tool. A tool to open doors to money, to push women to open themselves. He gets off on saying genuine things about his life and the feelings and validation that come from the pity and compassion that is shown, mostly by women. The men seem to smell his deception and growl and grimace when they stand behind him, listening, disrespecting him, all the while perplexed as to why his game seems to work ... at least some of the time.

He talks of trust and intimacy. It can't be faked, he says. Authenticity is all that matters. He picks the words of the person he's with and mirrors them, expands them, and parrots them back.

But certain sentences he recycles, knowing these particular ones serve to move his mission forward, an essential part of the prep work. He fails to realize that his voice changes from the repetition, becomes monotone from boredom with the tired phrases, the sales pitch that he needs to get through to close the deal. He's slipping a bit. He's aging and losing some of his polish and shine.

This latest woman is a surprise. (Aren't they all?) He finds her extraordinary, endlessly insightful. She has a soul, intelligence, the ability to touch and care for others. In moments, he sinks into it, allows himself to float away with the idea, the fantasy, of actually belonging somewhere, to someone. He feels like he's been awakened, hasn't ever felt like this. He hasn't experienced tenderness in years, maybe ever, has almost come to believe that kindness is elusive. He says he survives by burying himself in work.

Later, someone tells you he's survived by burying himself in women. That he doesn't even hide the string of conquests. His ego demands that he flaunt them to his peers.

He's on his way out of his marriage, he insists. It's inevitable. She only wants him for his money. He asks for concrete advice on his divorce, says it's been years in the making, and calls his wife "my unfortunate roommate." He hasn't been touched in a long time, at some point he must have the right to be intimate with someone else, *right*? Since he's leaving, after all, and it isn't really a marriage anyway, *right*? Can't even remember if there was ever a real connection. He should have known better than to pick such a shallow woman as "the wife." He uses strange, distancing language when he speaks of the woman he married.

He asks the new woman, the one who has awakened his soul, if he can see her in person soon.

In reality, he can hardly wait to close the deal, so he can move on to the next kill. This one has taken extra work.

He's been doing this for a long time, and he seems to have mastered the recipe. He feels like the greatest cook ever to have lived, right before the numbness and self-hatred settles into him again.

Sleep only comes with strong medication, to quiet the ever-chattering, cackling demons. *No matter*, he thinks, *everyone plays the game, I just play it better and win more often.* But somehow, somewhere, in the remnants of his childhood heart, he knows this isn't true.

That some people
love and give,
protect, soothe, and trust each other.

And *that*, he can hardly stand.

Because he knows
that you don't get love
like that in this lifetime
when you are utterly
unable to offer it.

. . .

This is written about a man I knew for a brief period of time. He tried and failed to seduce me, lying that he was divorcing and so wished to work with me. (Same man as in some of the other betrayal poems ... apparently I *really* needed to process this.)

His clients and connections were amazing. He was smart, funny, utterly charming, and incredibly good at sales. Lies leaked out of him constantly, which to me was both hurtful and fascinating. Life can be both. At least that's what I told myself as I was pulled into conversations that felt ickier and ickier. When I said no to a sexual relationship, but yes to the work ... the work vanished. Of course it did.

This man uses qualifiers when he lies and forgets his past fibs, so if you are paying attention, a new story often contradicts a previous one. After the initial contact, he prefers to attempt seduction via written word. He chooses messaging over face-to-face conversations or calls—it's much easier to create an illusion of intimacy that way— and he can quickly become busy when he panics or can't stomach what he's doing. Or if the woman he's playing guesses too much, too close to the truth. When I pushed for a verbal conversation, he would schedule calls with me and then not show up. It wasn't ever going to be a successful ruse, and yet, we both continued the conversations longer than we should have. It was foolishly dangerous for both of us.

The few times we saw each other in person were always in public settings, and interestingly, he boldly told me awful things about mutual connections. I came to believe that he was recounting the deviant behaviors of others in order to watch my face and vocal reactions to the deviant behaviors he himself engaged in.

On some level, he must have been desperate to learn what my opinion would be of his true self. He sometimes made me feel that in a different life we might have made a good match. But maybe that's the thing ... maybe his magic was that he could make every woman feel that way, at least fleetingly.

He seemed to have no idea how much information was seeping out of him, spilling past his figurative armor, dripping onto the floor, and making my feet so sticky I couldn't flee fast enough.

He's not healthy enough to talk about the real, the trauma, the actual and horrific abuse I know he endured. I recognized his broken bits at first glance, *in his first glance*. The pieces that were entirely beyond his control. Things no one should have to live through.

His trauma wouldn't have been a dealbreaker to me. However, his callousness and narcissism made us an impossible match.

I wonder whether he underestimated my skills while he played his "game," or if he just found it irresistible to go up against a worthy adversary. Maybe he hoped he would finally be caught. Maybe he could hardly stand the pain and numbness and simply wanted to be fully seen by someone who sees the broken bits in humans everywhere and shrugs it off and loves many shattered humans anyway.

How excruciating to watch a man so "skilled" in creating connection ultimately wield his power to use and abuse those who attempt to care for him. How very hard for his wife, from whom he wasn't actually separated. How utterly confusing for his children.

He is entirely untrustworthy in word and action because he so hates himself. I hope he gets some truly exceptional therapy. And finds a way to be a better man, more in line with who he pretends to be.

I won't hold my breath, but I'll say a prayer ... or three.

I firmly believe that despite the bad characters we encounter in life, it's important to stay able to choose optimism, kindness, and faith, since with functional people, we do indeed often receive what we give. And if we have friends and/or family members who are really good to us, we are better protected than we would otherwise be. How grateful I am to have a bubble of love around me.

My biggest, bestest love always tells me, "You can jump, Annie. I'll catch you. I'm always your soft place to land when you do hard, scary things."

And God. That makes all the difference in a life.

She makes every single bit of difference, to me.

Betrayal Behavior

S ometimes I wonder
why so many people
behave badly and then get angry at the person
who calls out the bad behavior

the problem isn't the talking about it
the problem is the betrayal behavior in the first place

I'm glad more people are speaking out
it's been such a long time coming, indeed

I was silenced
as a child,
as a teenager,
and as a young woman

I will not be silenced anymore

no more gaslighting
me or mine
no more
no more
no more

In particular, my childhood was covered in trying to shame me
for speaking up about the abuse inflicted upon me. No more.

No FUCKING more.

Sadness & Struggle

When I Write

When I write
I lean into it
let it pull me through the waves
of hurt and longing

I sink into it
and surrender
while it steals my sleep
and focus from all other things

except you

ever the center of the swirl
you and the Pandora's box
that you are attached to
that I *only* meant to peek at

turns out, that's not
how her box works

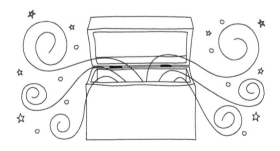

Bluff

I'm tired
from
the endless circle
of hope
love
and disappointment
you offer me

I know my goodbye
took you by surprise
and you thought
you had more time

I will always,
always love you
you're wired into me
imprinted in
indelible
ink

but this was *never platonic,*
not for a moment or a minute
not from your side,
not from mine

still, you punish yourself
with my memory,
planting yourself there

even though
my house no longer stands
and a white refrigerator-like beast
now sits abreast the
Bluff

you may live on it
but it will always be my
Street

"I think of you every time I pass your old house," he told me, years after he built his own a couple doors down from my childhood home.

"How often do you go past my old house?"

"Multiple times a day," he confessed.

• • •

Vulnerability[90] is on the chin. It's a piece of love, sadness, compassion, and empathy. For all of these emotions contain loss—or the understanding that loss is a possibility. It manifests on the chin in a tight squeeze and lift. It turns the chin, which usually looks like a soft, smooth grape, into a dimpled, shriveled raisin.

If you look into a mirror and have a hard time doing this, try clenching your butt. Then clench your chin in the same way. It's good when teaching concepts are ... memorable.

---

90   See #29 in the Glossary.

To Be Unseen

The Plague
brought with it
the weeping men

the lost
the lonely
the unloved

so, I listened and soothed and said, "No it's not me
I'm not the one
but I can hug you
and lament with you
that your marriage isn't what you thought it would be"

"I'm sorry," I said
"I know how hard that is
how isolating
and cruel
it feels to be unseen"

· · ·

We humans need to be seen and known to feel loved. It's why vulnerability and openness of heart are so necessary for true connection. If we don't show ourselves, we can't truly feel loved. And well, if we do show ourselves and we still aren't seen, we feel incredibly lonely.

Cracking

I cracked it, you know. Finally. That piece of loneliness that I told you I couldn't yet code.

All I needed was one look, one really good look at you, when I asked if you were okay, and there it was. The grayish flicker of unfocused emptiness in your charcoal eyes, right before you lied and said, "Good."

The lost, the numb, the dead look, the "refusal to participate fully in the living" look.

The focal blur in your irises and pupils. And with it, too, I saw the slant of skin from the outer corners of your eyes creating a faint line of sorrow, folded up toward the space between your brows. All of this fleeting before you recuperated and gained control. Your mask slipping for a nanosecond. Only.

There it was, the desolate look I've seen scarred into soldiers and bodyguards of dangerous men from foreign lands. The men who've seen others commit horrible acts, or who themselves have done abominable things, the visions of which continue to haunt them. Humans who have fully given up on humanity.

How strange to see it settled in you.

You, with whom I do connect. You, whom I see and who seems to see me. There have been moments, when we are surrounded by others, and you look at me as if maybe I can soothe every ache and every wound in you, even the self-inflicted ones.

And my trauma whispers to me to lean in and try. That I can do for you what no other person has been able to. And I *know*, I know, that that whisper in my brain is a lie.

That it comes from the broken parts of me. My desire to return to and fiddle with the messy, water-soaked puzzle pieces of my life, to create a different outcome
this time
re-live
re-live
re-live
and solve
this time
this time

I know you are but a stand-in, a carbon copy, who wants to bed me, add me to your list. Conquer yet another smart, competent, kind woman. You wouldn't, couldn't love me. Wouldn't bestow upon me the tenderness, kindness, and connection I so long for.

You are looking to get someone to switch your humanity back on. For you. You have nae the will, nor the strength to do it yourself.

I can't do it for you. I'm heartbroken for you (and for me), and for all of your pain. I see how deeply it runs, almost touching upon the shattered remnants of your childhood heart. The pieces of you that you so firmly resolve are unwanted, unloved.

You won't find the solution outside of your own bruised and battered skin.

So, as it turns out,
it wasn't exactly loneliness that I saw in you,
not in the common sense
but in the beaten, broken sense,
the eternal and alone,
by-the-self sense,
I guess it also was.

...

I was so lonely when I met this man that I initially ignored the warning signals. For some reason, he pressed some of my very old trauma buttons, the ones that go all the way back to childhood.

I've come to believe that what I initially thought was loneliness in him was more specifically disassociating. This desolate state is the manifestation of removing oneself from the world, from people, time, and space. It's important with facial expressions not to jump to conclusions about the source of the emotion. The feeling can be clear as day, but the "why" may remain unclear. However, revisiting certain topics with the person while watching their facial expressions can provide more clues.

That said, I'm going to give some examples of what this gaze may indicate ... Sometimes when I've identified this look, I've later found out that the person has survived sexual abuse.

However, I rarely see this gaze in people who have experienced sexual trauma AND received really good therapy. Many of those people become extra protective of others. We humans do have an amazing ability to be both scarred and mostly healed. And some exceptional humans use their trauma to try to make sure others don't have to endure similar experiences.

Except for when I'm teaching children to recognize predatory behavior, my work isn't focused on security. I do recognize deep trauma, but no, it's not my business to pull an individual out and try to figure out what their troubles stem from. And frankly, there are simply too many of us who are traumatized to even begin such work. A sad state indeed that we all tend to think we are alone in it. Most of the time, when I see trauma, I'll wish you well and add you to my prayers.

That said, if *you* see someone who exhibits this gaze, the dead look in the eyes, be extra cautious. If it feels safe and comfortable to do so, encourage them to seek professional help.

And please, keep them away from your children. You don't need to be able to scientifically dissect something to know something is "off" with another human. Don't take risks with your children or yourself when your body warns you about someone or something. Our primitive brains know things that we can't necessarily put into words.

Remember that humans can be dangerous, regardless of gender and regardless of age.

Pay particular attention to your own needs and neediness. We are more likely to ignore warning signs when we feel lonely. Spending time with people who love us and make us laugh is the best antidote.

Writing

Writing is hard,
solitary,
involuntary

it leaks out of me
in the most inopportune
of times,
but I can't help it

Conflict Avoidance

Ghosting
is the laziest
most inconsiderate way
to show that you are so much less than I need you to be

but it does, at least, get the point across

why *not* just light the fuse and run?
so far that you can't even hear the quiet explosion
of disappointment
inside my heart

(I get that your anxiety rules you. That doesn't make it okay.
You should get help with that.)

Not a Pretzel

M e staying small, wasn't ever going to be an option
I'm too bold,
too smart, to twist myself
into a pretzel
just to please you

if I've learned anything in life
it's how to move and wiggle free
despite
the scars on my heart

Etched into Your Skin

E very time I see you
there is less of you

the grief that was etched into your skin is making way
for a lost look
age has made me powerful
but the years have weakened you,
eroded you, and left me
with so little of you

I would have come back for you, you know?
if you hadn't closed all the windows
and left one open, instead of bolting every single one shut
and yet, you ultimately succumbed (as did I)
and you planted yourself permanently, solidly,
only two doors down
in a vase,
built of glass, a bubble of ice

I wondered how you did it,
kept everyone oblivious to our pain?
pain, that was written, is still written
pain
plain as day, obvious in the movements of your face,
now etched deeply
into the wrinkles

on your face

• • •

I can look at the placement of the wrinkles on someone's face and
see which emotions they've shown over and over. Like water carving
valleys, the constant repetition of a specific emotion leaves undeniable
traces of our emotional lives, wrinkled and scraped into our skin.

Breadcrumbing Me

You give only enough to keep
the attachment
I watch how you do it in work
and in love

we are friends, you say,
as you use me for your work
you so love the attention of my brain
and the affection of my childish heart

and yet
and yet
it isn't ever *my* turn

my messages go unanswered
(unless you need something)

my calls unreturned
(until you want something)

you offer a trail of breadcrumbs
thin
unsatisfying
leaving much to be desired

I bring you a feast every time we meet
I plan it, ponder it, pick out the bits that will
fill your tummy, your brain, your soul
I give in abandon, abundance
and affection

I defend you, protect you,
teach you my magic
things that only I know

I offer you insight when no one else shares
tell you only the truth when your disciples lie
and yet
and yet
you offer crumbs
and sometimes not even

how are you possibly surprised?
when I say goodbye
adieu, farewell

I'm famished
but no longer for nourishment
from you

soon I will stop worrying about your
impoverished heart

soon … soon
almost
for sure

• • •

This piece is about a couple people in my life who elicited in me a similar feeling of sadness and frustration around the same time.

Learning not only how to create alliances, but also how to strengthen and maintain them *matters*, not just in friendship and work, but also in well-being.

He's Freezing and I'm Confetti

He's stuck in a freeze response
due to trauma

and if I were normal, regular, more appropriately wired ...
I'd probably respect that and give him space

but nope,
I'm a box of confetti

I leap and joke and pour an abundance of affection
allllll over him
to make him laugh,
to warm his toes and
rub his heart, and
to move, manually, the blood through his veins

breathe,
breathe,
breathe,
pump,
pump,
pump

because I love him so,
and need him to remain with me on this earth
and to do that his heart needs to
beat,
beat,
beat

so he can
stay,
stay,
stay

even when I'm crabby,

stay

...

Anguish[91] has a similar lower face to that of grief, but to the extreme. The bottom corners of the mouth pull diagonally down and out toward the outside corresponding shoulders. The chin puckers, and this squeezing pushes the center of the bottom lip up and out. Grief and anguish are both mixed expressions: with building blocks from fear (the rectangular mouth) and from sadness (the puckered chin). I see anguish as larger and more intense than grief—meaning the chin will be more puckered and the bottom lip more stretched into a rectangular shape.

Both grief and anguish are often accompanied by touching the face. To sooth, calm, and provide—even minimum—relief. Sometimes anguish is further expressed by looking up to the sky and praying for help with outstretched hands and fingers.

Remember, if a man has a beard, we still know his chin is puckering, even if we can't see the skin, because it causes his bottom lip to protrude.

---

91   See #23 in the Glossary.

The Doofus

"I like it when you call me Doofus"

"Well ... if the Doo fits"

I'm sad for you,
but feeling better as I nail
the window shut again
and paint over the bits
where the hammer stains the wood
with its concave scars

our truth is
stranger and stronger and sadder
than fiction

forged in steel I am,
at least
that's what I tell myself
as I miss you

Untouched

" I haven't been touched in years," my friend told me. "I'm scared to leave the mother of my child. I don't love her, and she doesn't love me. Our child has never even seen us hold hands."

"How do you manage? No one touches you?" I ask, my heart breaking for him.

"I touch myself, soothe myself. You get used to it, the misery, it settles in you and feels familiar. But it's good to hear your voice, the warmth of my old friend who knows me and loves me and makes me feel seen.

It helps, a bit at least.

I think, at some point when my son is older, and his mother can no longer take him from me, that I'll leave. I'll go and then maybe there will be a piece of happiness left for me to still find in this life.

Meanwhile, tell me of your adventures across the sea, your insightful, silly, salty stories. Read me your writings and help me to drift away on your voice,

if only for a moment."

To Write Well

To write well
(as to love well)

I need to bypass
my rational brain
not so much to put myself
in a mood ... no, it's more of
a state

sleeplessness helps,
drunk without alcohol,
a me I'd prefer others not to see
exhausted, delirious, and
wide-awake

Cake

I always saved you the last piece
of cake, but
you never
saved any cake
for me

Can't be Drunk and Guarded

A taxi driver once told me that everyone in his country must drink. "You can't be drunk and guarded, so if you don't drink, you must be police."

So, forgive my emotional nakedness, if I'm inappropriate and unfiltered. It's necessary to be emotionally drunk, fully saturated, and unguarded to teach.

And really, *it can't go both ways.*

In order to do my profession well, I need to show the full, long, large expressions, over and over. Fear, the NO Face, Anger, Sorrow, Aggression, Love, Kindness, Joy, Holding Back, Knowing Smiles ...

Inevitably, my body and mind believe the roller coaster is real. My brain processes the emotion that I'm showing on my face as true and real and now. Indeed, this is how brains are wired. After a workshop, my brain and body think I've experienced the negative emotions that an average person might experience over a period of many months.

An emotional hangover and excruciating loneliness settle into me and last at least a day or two. The only way I've found to expunge it is by removing it manually. Press it out with long, tight hugs, belly laughing, snuggling in close to a loved one. Ninety-minute massages help to rub out the sorrow. Or, if nothing else is available, tears allow a bit of release.

The only way I know how to teach emotion well is by exhibiting, which means removing every cloak of self-protection, leaving me raw, vulnerable, needy. It's only temporary. And my time to do it, finite.

The chill of nakedness
bearable only because
I need to protect others,
in a way that I wasn't
protected myself.

• • •

Aggression[92] and hate are names for the RUN! Face. This complex expression shows that the person making it is ready to verbally or physically attack another person. It includes a furrowed brow, squinty eyelids, and popping eyeballs—all which show anger. The nose wrinkles, lifted lip, and nostril shadows show the NO Face. Tight lips with a "gonna get you!" mouth that reaches out toward the intended victim show extreme aggression.

It took me a long time to come to terms with teaching emotions to anyone other than my children, partly because my brain feels so well suited for strategic advisory, and I was reluctant to give up that mental chess game.

My master's degree in anthropology and my experience performing strategic advisory work across industries, countries, and in multiple languages gives me an edge in correctly assessing complex political landscapes. I believe kindness is underused in business, and I am skilled at finding solutions that protect and unify as well as include, rather than exclude. Many of my clients over the years have been family offices where people aren't treated as disposable, and where you are stuck with each other—so you'd better make it work.

For so many years, I chose to hide my ability to read expressions and detect lies. My clients knew I had *something*. They just didn't know what it was.

---

92   See #26 in the Glossary.

Moving from focusing on mostly the brain to mostly emotion was initially an overwhelming endeavor. And yet, it feels more meaningful with every passing year.

However, teaching emotions keeps me in the rawer, more sensitive parts of my brain and heart and comes at more of a physical cost to my body chemistry than strategy work ever did.

Untangling

I remember finally letting go of him, how my body uncoiled even in sleep, the release palpable as my arms unfurled, uncurled, and stretched, one finally reaching to hang over the side of the bed, the other straight out to the side ...

Instead of twisted in tight like a pretzeled snake, desperate to find solace in my own skin with my hands on my face, or coiled tight at my neck, or folded into the skin at the top of my chest when I slept. All forcing stiffness and ache into muscles, wrists and shoulders, hips and back from the winding and pulling of my body into a wound ball.

untangling him from my heart
allowing me to
stretch and reach out
into the space around me
soaking into the release and relief
of giving him up

and I know, I *know,*
it's etched deeply in me
and will reappear at some point
   but until then
      I rest

· · ·

We rub our own skin when we feel the need to calm down. We touch it when we are wound up, nervous, scared, insecure, worried, etc. If you ask me about this and I'm comfortable with you, I will tell you that I believe it goes back to breastfeeding. What we really want is someone else's soft, warm skin to press against, to soothe the hurt. The breast that once provided comfort, nourishment, love, and safety.

Lately, many people have asked me why they sleep curled into a ball and/or with a hand on their face, or on their neck tucked tightly down toward their cleavage. It's because when we don't feel relaxed or safe, we use whatever resources we have to help calm ourselves down. Sometimes that means sleeping close into a loved one or a pet or hugging a pillow. And sometimes it means touching our own skin because that's the only skin that is available. Unfortunately, the more tightly we wrap ourselves into a ball, the more we wake up stiff and achy.

Fluster & Hope

I Make You Rowdy

"You're embarrassed because I make you rowdy."

"I do not get rowdy. I'm a grown man."

"Noooooo you aren't. Not with me. You're all polished and poised with new people, but I still make you silly. *I still make you young.*"

"It does feel good to be young again," he sighed, tilted his head, and showed me his gentle love smile. The one he held back so often when we were young.

"Remember when I used to lick my finger and stick it in your ear to make you jump?"

"That was sooooo irritating!"

"I know. You're like my own personal jack-in-the-box, and I love making you jump. Wind, wind, wind. PA! BOOM! Sooo fun!"

"I'm glad that I ... please you?" His voice low and gravelly as his pupils dilated and his gaze moved down my neck and lingered on my breasts.

"You do. You really do."

• • •

The **love smile**[93] is my favorite smile. It took me years to figure out why certain photos were "touching" to me in a way that others weren't. Years of watching faces around me with expressions filled with gentle affection that *moved me differently.* Years of trying to put the pieces together.

The love smile always has a closed mouth. A rise of the cheeks pulls up and stretches the corners of the mouth into a gentle, soft smile filled

---

93   See #14, #15, and #16 in the Glossary.

with affection. When you reach the place where you can feel this smile on your own face as it is happening, it adds a whole other level to the endorphins already flooding you.

I differentiate between the love smile, which has a piece of joy in it, and straight-up joy.

In pure **joy**,[94] the cheeks lose gravity and rise up high, forcing the skin just below the lower eyelashes to pop out. These are the smile bags, and they are beautiful! There are few things in life that we humans like more than having someone look at us while showing us their smile bags.

If you're unclear on visualizing this, think of the skin under your eyes that gets brown or purplish—depending on your skin tone and pigment—when you are overtired. That sideways half-circle is what gets fat and jolly and oh-so-delightful. Joy is contagious.

Bliss.

Note that you can show a facial expression of joy with or without a smile of the mouth. I look for smile bags *rather than looking at the mouth* to get a proper read on whether a person is really happy.

And yes, I feel every single facial expression that I make. And, no, I can't switch off my ability to see them on others' faces or to feel them on my own face.

---

94   See #11 in the Glossary.

Flustered

R ight now
flustered is my new favorite emotion
especially
when it comes on the face of a man
who is almost never
anymore

and it comes with arousal,
yours, for me
especially
when it makes you stutter with your expressions,
your words, your want

when you're trying to drink your drink
and you almost spit it out,
because I've said something wickedly inappropriate
and oh so funny,
and you know that it means
I'm teasing you and tempting you,
which you like so very much, indeed
because it reminds you
that I want you so

I'm working
on pulling apart the pieces of the expression
so I may need to incite it, invite it,
from you
some more

tempt me
and I will,
my Love

tempt me
and I will

The Most

When you are scared,
    you make assumptions
I know that's deep in your muscle memory,
but maybe you could just ask ...
and I'll remind you that
I love you
the Most

• • •

It matters so very much to us humans to be somebody's favorite. Especially in romantic love, and especially when life has been harder than anticipated. I told him very late in the day that he's been mine. Always.

In my lifetime,
he is mine.

Why I Write the Truth

When I was deciding what to write in this book, I made the decision to focus on what I would have wanted to know in my twenties and, more specifically, what I would want my children's friends and loved ones to know. The things that I have tried so hard to teach my own children, day after day, year after year.

So, I've written my truth with as much specificity as I can.

I hope learning to read expressions helps you make safe and healthy decisions about whom to trust and whom to partner with when it comes to platonic, romantic, and professional relationships.

I also hope it helps you trust your gut when it comes to seeing who around you needs extra love and kindness and whom to *absolutely stay away from*.

May you learn some of the lessons early,
that I learned so late in life.

And may you always know others,
by their true hearts,
and by the expressions on their faces.

I pray that I have taught you well
and may God watch over you, always.

Thank Yous

Thank you to all the people who loved and lifted me in the writing of this book:

Emma FJ for loving me better than anyone in my lifetime and for waiting on the other side to catch me, both to celebrate and to tend to my wounds. Thank you for using your brilliant mind and beautiful heart to help me put words on hard things.

Rick M for loving me our whole lives with your whole face. Thank you for encouraging me to write our story and for wanting every piece to be about you. I will always love you too.

Carrington W for holding me tight in your heart and for going first and modeling brave and kind, time and time again. Through all my flaws, my sass, and my silly, I know I can tell you everything, and you will find in it the softness and humor every time.

Kate E who should be everyone's first pick in love and war. You make Glencoe still feel like home.

Marie O who knows that making someone laugh is one of the best ways to love them. Your endlessly dirty humor is the best in my lifetime. I'm always happier after spending time with you and your huge heart.

Susan B for your intelligence, wit, and compassion. I'm so grateful for our similar wiring and lifelong connection. You have the gift your father had of making others feel truly seen and loved.

Ashley Mc for all the talks about humans, their behavioral patterns and motivations, and for always laughing at my jokes. You are amazing at lifting other people up. Love you.

Eva O for decades of unfiltered friendship and endless personal and professional support.

Björn for constantly showing up with kindness, insight, and fun. There is no story I won't repeat to make you howl with laughter. I throw myself into shenanigans just to be able to entertain you afterward with the story.

Rob, Suzanne, and T for making me feel like family. I'm still giggling at Robby's, "Not that it's any of my business, *but can I just ask ...*" My life is always your business, and I can't think of anything I wouldn't tell you three.

ER for loving me and my kids.

Andrea O for always telling me your truth, for making me laugh, and for decades of friendship.

Boris and Ylva for 10 years of "write the book!" and for always cheerfully clearing your schedules when I arrive in Sweden, no matter how unexpectedly.

D for understanding that love means being brave and doing hard things. For your unfiltered friendship, and for how you protect and lift up your loved ones.

Beth T for your friendship through this bumpy piece of middle age, for loving my writing and screaming in delight when I read you my good poems.

Lotta L for loving me even when I'm far away, and for teaching me to never allow sorrow to build a nest inside me. Älskar Dig.

Nathan for telling me to write the truth and for your extreme kindness in the early stages of my divorce. The big things matter too.

Elena B for the many real and heartfelt phone calls during the recent transitions of my life. And for believing that the world needs my work.

Claire R for worrying about me through the writing process and helping me to clarify that I only wanted to write the truth.

Grace N for the constant encouragement and support for my book and my heart. And for pushing me to be brave and bold whenever I need a little extra nudge. I'm so grateful to have you as a friend.

Marta for knowing my truth from the beginning like no one else. It is truly a gift to be seen, understood, and supported.

Kelly B for your unflinching belief in me and for putting me on my first huge stage to teach facial expressions, knowing that this one event would change my life. Thank you.

Liz K and Kris S for your beautiful hearts, abandoned laughter, and willingness to speak so honestly about your lives. For always including me and making me feel like I'm doing you the favor when I visit. Love you both.

Dr. Matthew Henry for inspiring me with your sublime, raw, and real poetry and for helping me with my writings and early drafts.

Sarah Mattern, my designer, illustrator, advisor, and now also my friend. Everything you touch becomes a work of art. I'm so grateful that you choose to share your gifts with me.

Barry Braunstein for his beautiful studio photography. I'm so thankful for your generosity, collaboration, and ability to make me laugh so I could be comfortable showing the range of emotions we needed to capture. Your work is spectacular.

Amy Waninger for helping with editing and offering the perfect balance of soft, firm, and funny to help me to be as bold as I need to be to publish my diary. You were the right professional and the right friend to come into my life at the right time.

The women of Brown Ledge Camp who helped raise me and continue to love me, and each other, *well.* For teaching me that women always support other women; it's how we love, and who we are. This has made every bit of difference in my life.

The friends and loved ones of my children, I am grateful for how unfiltered you all are when you tell your stories and your giggles make the walls of my house shake. It makes life so much better to embrace the real and ridiculous in life. I love you, and may God bless you all.

And finally, thank you to my Lovies: Lea, Emma, and Matthias for a lifetime of love, laughter, and insightful conversations about humans and faces. My greatest joy is appreciating the tenderness and awkwardness of humanity together with you. I'm so proud of your beautiful hearts. May God bless and keep you always.

Real and authentic
is so very much better than
poised, polished, and pretend.
Also, it's much funnier.

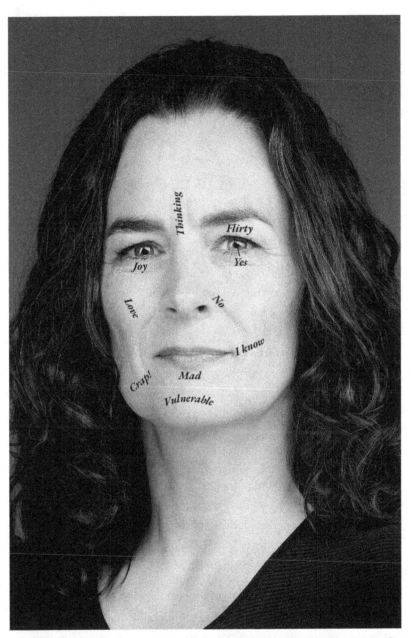

FACIAL EXPRESSIONS
GLOSSARY

Overview

What follows is a visual guide to the world of the nonverbal and universal language of our species. All the facial expressions I teach here show on our faces, regardless of age, gender, socialization, culture, or geographic location.

Facial expressions are a teachable skill because we humans have biological responses to emotions. Each emotion creates a specific and different change in blood flow and muscle movement. We are also hardwired to emotionally respond to facial expressions when we see them on other people's faces.

This glossary includes clean and marked up photographs of each facial expression, accompanied by descriptions. As you study these expressions, try making them yourself in a mirror to gauge what emotions you see and feel. The practice of making expressions is needed for the brain to fully process and interpret them. *This is how we are wired!* **If you want to test yourself**, skip the glossary table of contents and look at each picture to first see if you can determine the primary emotion (yes, some of them have hints of other feelings) and then turn the page to see if you got it right!

Note that this glossary includes both full and fleeting expressions. Full expressions contain all the pieces of the specific emotion on the face. They are also usually held for a bit. Duration and the wholeness of the expression make them easier to see. Fleeting or partial expressions can be harder to identify if your gaze isn't prepared, or if you don't understand the expression's primary location on the face.

I've worked for years with my daughters and son to identify what we consider the primary location on the face for each specific emotion. This has helped us identify expressions even when only using our peripheral vision—if you see a jump, or a sudden movement in the primary location of that emotion/expression, you can identify the feeling, even when you have a less-than-clear view and your eye only catches a flicker or a jolt.

We know, for example, that a jump on the chin is vulnerability, a flash of the white area in the eyes above the irises is fear, and a jolt next to the nostril is "No!"

With enough practice in the mirror, study of the photographs here, watching other people's faces, and working with videos (look up my videos online), it is possible to actually feel an expression as it pops up on your face. To me, this feels like a tiny sting of electricity localized to a specific area of the face.

As for seeing expressions on others, get used to planting your gaze on the lower face around the mouth or the glabella (the space between the eyebrows). In particular, be ready to look at either of these areas when you know you want to gauge another person's response to something you're going to ask or say.

Personally, I favor watching the lower part of the face. Though I look at the entire face, I always go back and forth from direct eye contact to the area around the mouth when I'm talking to someone.

Note—do not stare more than three seconds at a time at someone's mouth while they are looking back at you. Their brain will tell them that you want to kiss them. I may have learned this the hard way. Ugh!

However, if their gaze is on another person and you are off to the side, you can look at their mouth area as long as you like.

Practice watching expressions in videos and set your gaze on the lower part of the face. Play, pause, rewind, watch in slow motion, and try watching without sound.

The studio photographs included here were shot by the exceptional Barry Braunstein. I've included my own informal, personal photographs for emotions that can be difficult to capture in a studio setting, particularly those involving unbridled joy, pleasure, happiness, love, relief, flirting, and desire. I've used real pictures for these because I can't make these expressions on demand—I need to actually be feeling the emotion in the moment. For each of these photos, I remember exactly what I was feeling.

If you want to test yourself...

Skip the glossary table of contents and look at each picture to see if you can determine the primary emotion (yes, some of them have hints of other feelings).

Then turn the page to see if you got it right!

Contents

Guess the expression! Then turn the page. ⟶

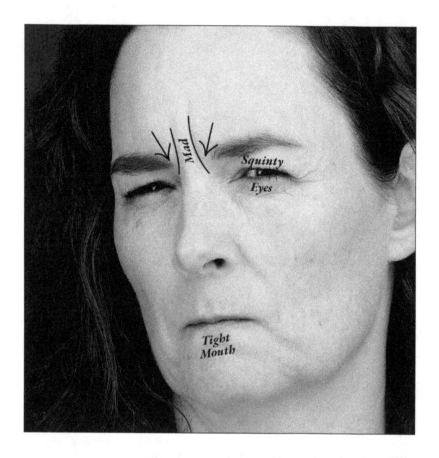

1. Anger

In this expression, the brows pull tightly toward each other and down toward the nose tip. Since this same brow movement exists in deep thinking, look for proof of anger in tight lips. Lips may also be pushed out like they are trying to grab at something, or they may be puckered and/ or closed tight—but either way, they will be TIGHT if anger is present. Anger may also be shown in bulging eyes or squeezed muscles around the eyes.

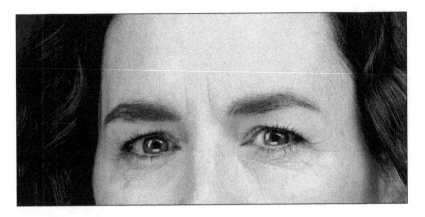

Guess the expression! Then turn the page. ⟶

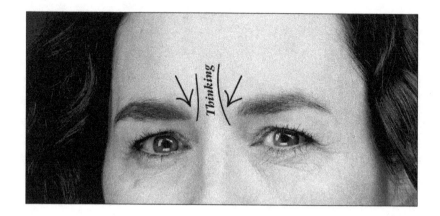

2. Deep Thinking (solving problems)

Deep thinking includes the same furrowed brow as anger—so the forehead looks identical, but the lips won't be tight. If the lips *are* tight, that's evidence of anger. A furrowed brow gives me wrinkles that I call my parentheses—I have two very clear, vertical lines that are visible even when my face is relaxed. These two wrinkles are etched into skin from years of repetitively making this expression. Some people only have one clear wrinkle between their eyebrows.

Guess the expression! Then turn the page. ⟶

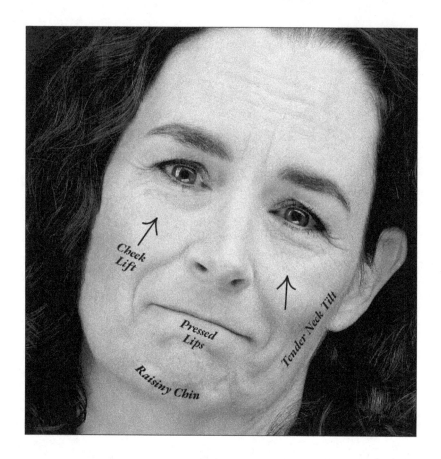

3. Empathy, Compassion, Kindness

Empathy, compassion, and kindness show in a puckered, raisiny chin accompanied by lifted cheeks. This is the look of "I see your pain, and I'm sending you support and kindness." Note that sometimes I also feel empathy in my heart and on my face simply by mirroring whatever expressions the other person is exhibiting. If they are angry, I may show anger on their behalf, etc. I often find myself nodding to show understanding as they are telling their story. This photograph shows extra softness in the tenderness of the head tilt.

Guess the expression! Then turn the page. $\longrightarrow$

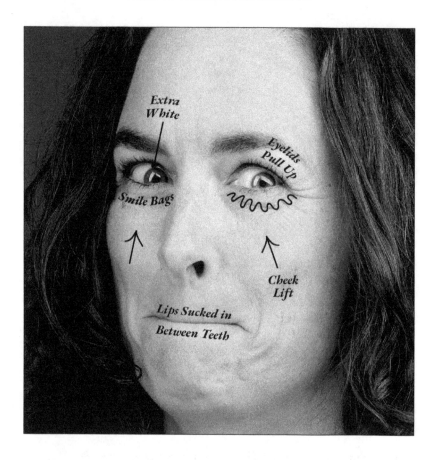

4. Excitement, Mischief

In excitement, lifted cheeks create smile bags under the eyes showing joy, and sucked-in lips show playful mischief. Both upper and lower eyelids pull up—BUT if the eyelids are pulled up *too* hard above the irises, this signifies fear—so, if the attempted excitement is disingenuous, it ends up signaling danger. (Think Hilary Clinton's expression when she tries to feign excitement. When the eyelids are pulled way up, and signaling fear is completely out of context, it makes people feel uncomfortable and like something is "off.")

Guess the expression! Then turn the page. $\longrightarrow$

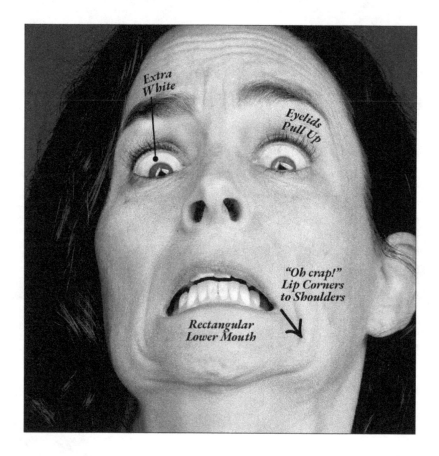

5. Fear

In fear, the lower lip forms a rectangle, the upper eyelids pull way back to show the white space above the irises, and the eyebrows pull straight up. Fear makes the neck tendons jump, stretch, and pop. Whenever I see a jolt of neck tendons, I know it's fear. I find this to be one of the tells that is visible even with only peripheral vision.

Guess the expression! Then turn the page. $\longrightarrow$

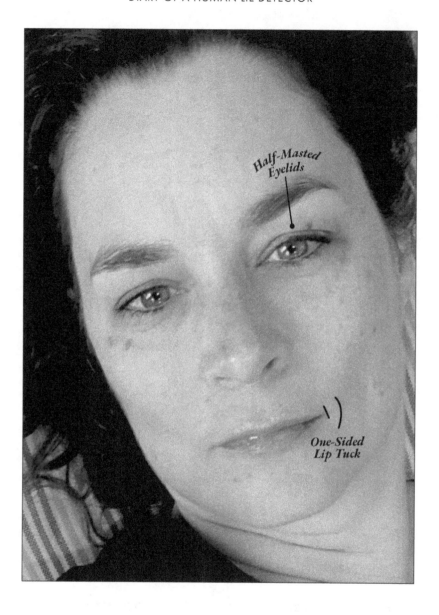

Half-Masted Eyelids

One-Sided Lip Tuck

6. Flirty A

In this personal photograph, I'm showing flirty eyes, or bedroom eyes, by lowering and "half-masting" my eyelids. There is a hint of a knowing smile—the Mona Lisa smile—which pulls one corner of the lips slightly up and tucks it into the cheek.

Guess the expression! Then turn the page. $\longrightarrow$

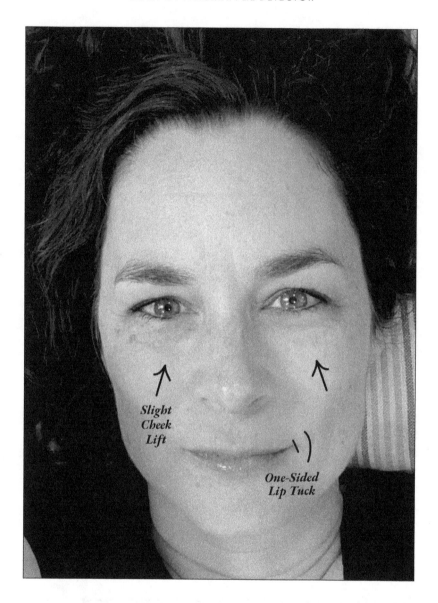

Slight Cheek Lift

One-Sided Lip Tuck

7. Flirty B

When feeling flirty, the corners of the mouth can slightly raise, and one lip corner often tucks into the cheek. In this personal photograph, I'm trying to do a neutral expression, but I still have a bit of a knowing smile as well as a slight intensity in the eyes. I'd just woken up from a particularly vivid dream.

Guess the expression! Then turn the page. ⟶

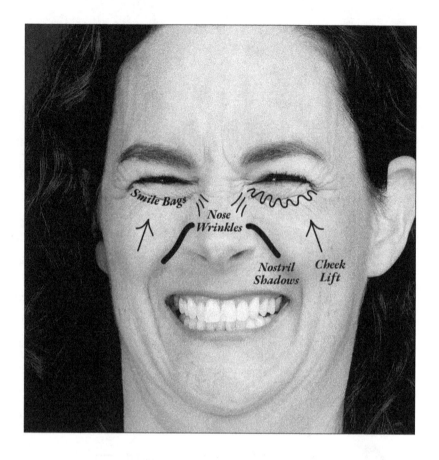

8. Funny and Inappropriate (the dirty joke expression)

This is a complex expression with two feelings presenting together to form an emotional sentence. Joy's raised cheeks and the resulting smile bags, combined with the NO Face's nostril shadows and squished wrinkles on the sides of the nose, express delight in the uncomfortable. This is the face I make, for example, when someone says something wickedly inappropriate and also very funny. The smile is slightly exaggerated here—probably because I was a bit uncomfortable making the expression on demand. That said, this expression usually has a piece of "awkward" in it, so that's not a bad thing!

Guess the expression! Then turn the page. $\longrightarrow$

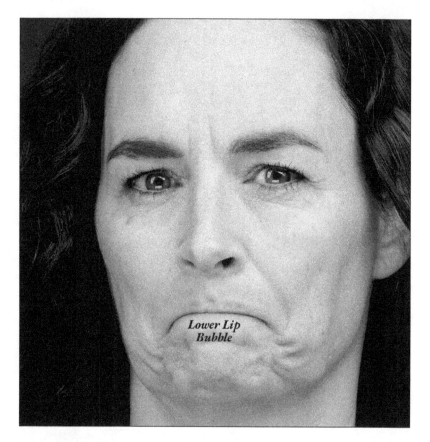

Lower Lip Bubble

9. Holding Back

This is a big expression, rather than a small or fleeting expression. There's a bubble below the bottom lip—what I sometimes call the Nordic chewing-tobacco bubble, because when I lived in Sweden, I knew a few people who, instead of tucking their chewing tobacco under their top lip, would tuck it between their lower teeth and lower lip. It takes effort to get the lower lip to pull in and down, and the chin has to move up to force out that bubble of skin (don't confuse the resulting chin pucker with vulnerability). This is the grown-up version of a child holding their hands over their mouth so they won't leak a secret. Think of it as the, "I have something to say and am bursting to tell you, but I don't want to get in trouble" look. In my experience, a person with this expression will usually share their thoughts once they are in a more comfortable environment—since they are already itching to say it!

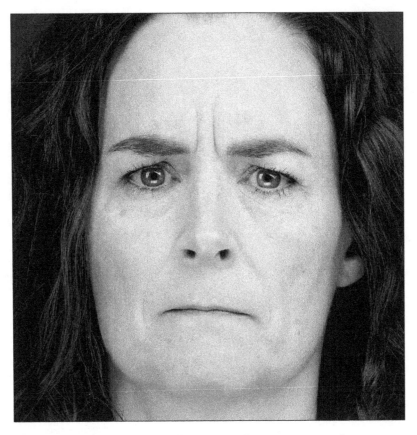

Guess the expression! Then turn the page. $\longrightarrow$

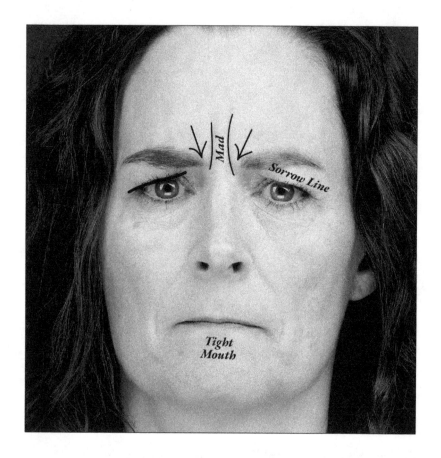

10. Hurt

The facial expression of hurt includes the sorrow lines and puckered chin of sadness and vulnerability, along with the furrowed brow and tight mouth of anger.

Guess the expression! Then turn the page. $\longrightarrow$

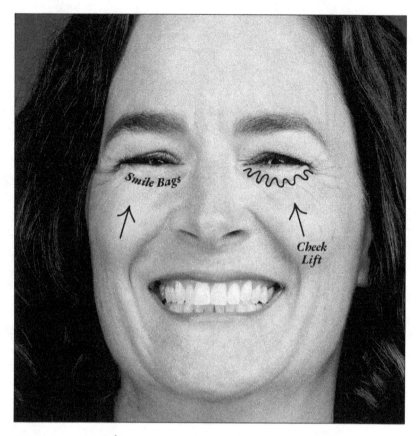

11. Joy, Pleasure, Happiness

In real joy, the cheeks lose gravity—they rise and push the skin under the lower eyelids out because it has nowhere to go. This bulging occurs in the area underneath our eyes where we get dark circles from fatigue. I call these smile bags, and they are usually accompanied by a shadow under the bulge of skin that looks like a sideways crescent moon.

It is my stout and firm belief that we humans attach more to others who show their smile bags often. It is ironic that so many people want to do away with their smile bags and remove them from photos, when really they are one of the most attractive pieces of human expression. Simply put, happiness is healing and appealing, and showing our humanity is beautiful.

The following personal photographs also show joy and happiness.

Guess the expression! Then turn the page. $\longrightarrow$

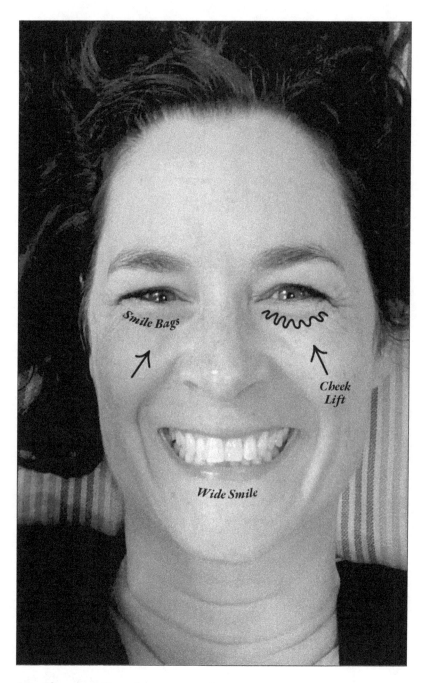

Joy, Pleasure, Happiness

Guess the expression! Then turn the page. $\longrightarrow$

Joy, Pleasure, Happiness

Guess the expression! Then turn the page. ⟶

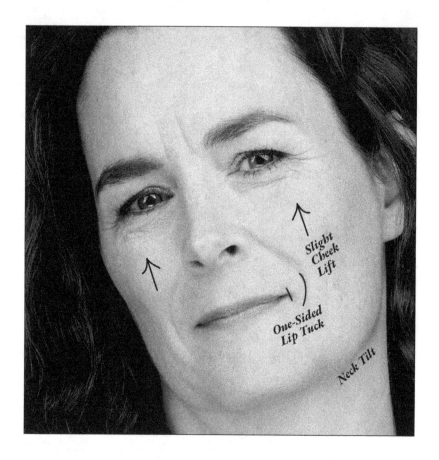

12. Knowing Smile (kind)

"I know something I think you don't know I know." (Yeah, I know!) This is a one-sided smile that has a soft, often kind or even loving look if the cheeks are raised. I also call this the Mona Lisa smile. It's often made in a discussion where someone is talking about something that the other person is well versed in. When it appears in flirtation, there will be other indicators, such as raised cheeks, lowered eyelids, and/or dilated pupils—in that case, it can also be interpreted as the "I know what you want, Baby!" look.

Guess the expression! Then turn the page. ⟶

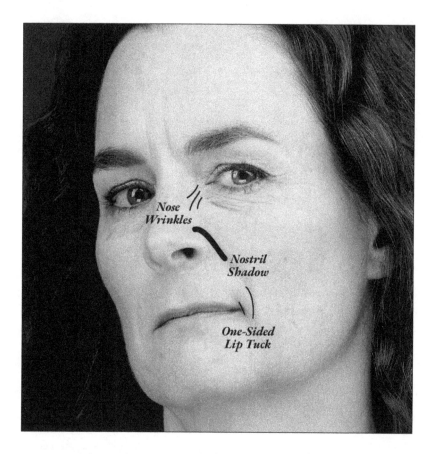

Nose Wrinkles

Nostril Shadow

One-Sided Lip Tuck

13. Knowing Smile (sinister)

This smile is similar to the knowing smile in that it has one lip corner tucked deep into the cheek—but the sinister knowing smile ALSO has a nostril shadow. It is the nostril shadow that turns this expression into one of ill intent. The nostril shadow will present on the same side of the face as the tucked lip. If you have a hard time catching the nostril shadow in a fleeting expression, trust your gut. Did it feel creepy, dirty, or unkind? If so, then it is a sinister knowing smile.

Be careful—particularly if the sinister knowing smile is accompanied by kind words. A facial expression that is the opposite of a person's words shows deception. Think of a fairytale where an evil character has a sinister expression while saying "come hither" words. Be wary! The sinister knowing smile can show predatory intent.

Guess the expression! Then turn the page. $\longrightarrow$

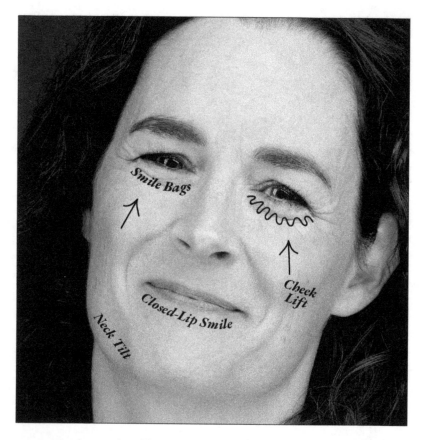

14. Love (affection)

This is the affectionate love smile. I make this expression when I'm with the people I care deeply for. It can simply express a soft, platonic love, as in the photo above, and have none of the additional elements that are present in romantic love. Romantic elements would include pupil dilation, half-masted eyelids, and flushed skin. In both affection and romance, the love smile has a head tilt and a soft lift of the cheeks, which pushes out smile bags under the eyes and pulls up a gentle, closed-lipped smile. It may also include a puckered chin showing vulnerability—I do this expression often when I look at my children and feel that time is moving too fast. The puckering is hard to see in this expression because of the stretching of the chin from the smile piece. Sometimes there is also a soft, downward *contrasting* pull of the lip corners almost like in mirth—as if love carries with it a soft secret.

Guess the expression! Then turn the page. ⟶

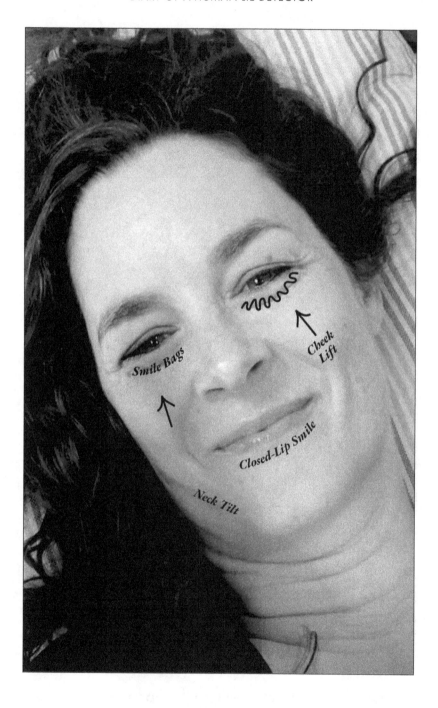

15. Love (romantic) A

This is a complex expression that I believe is almost impossible to fake. All the pieces together build a paragraph of romantic love, which, when authentic, is a combination of joy, vulnerability, softness, flirtation, and arousal.

A gentle tilt of my head shows a willingness to be soft and vulnerable. My eyelids are relaxed and lowered in flirtation and desire. There is joy expressed in my raised cheeks and bulging of the skin under my lower eyelids. My "love smile" shows in my closed lips, which are stretched from the upwards-and-outwards pull of my cheeks. The love smile always feels *soft*, and when I make it on my own face, it floods my body with endorphins. It was bright when this picture was taken, so my impression is that my pupils are somewhat dilated, though it's hard to tell.

Another piece you should look for in this expression is the chin puckered in tenderness. That's harder to see with a smile, but proves that the emotion is strong and there is a willingness to be vulnerable. Look also to see if the skin is flushed with arousal—a flush is likely associated with desire if you see the skin color change in front of you, accompanied by pupil dilation and half-masting the eyelids.

Guess the expression! Then turn the page. $\longrightarrow$

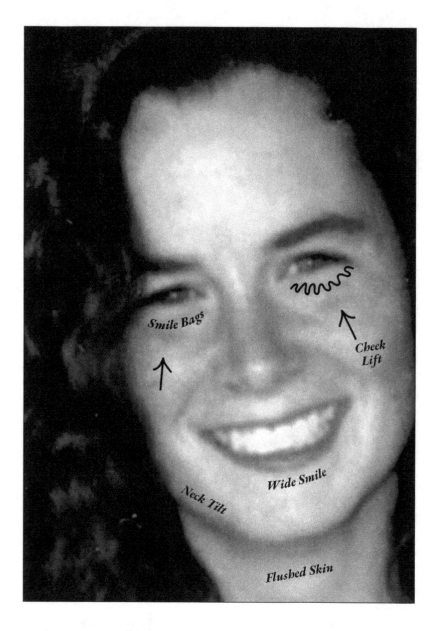

16. Love (romantic) B

This photo, as well as the next one, both show *in*-love, aroused, and deeply happy. This expression has the same neck tilt, raised cheeks, smile bags as the previous, but the skin is flushed with desire. The smile is open and wide.

Guess the expression! Then turn the page. $\longrightarrow$

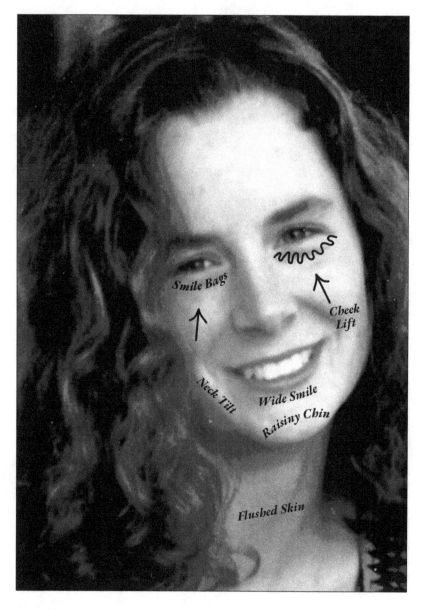

Love (romantic)

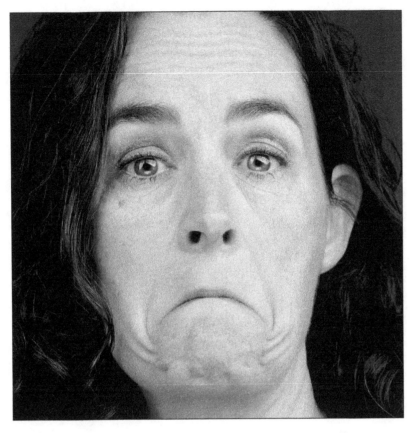

Guess the expression! Then turn the page. ⟶

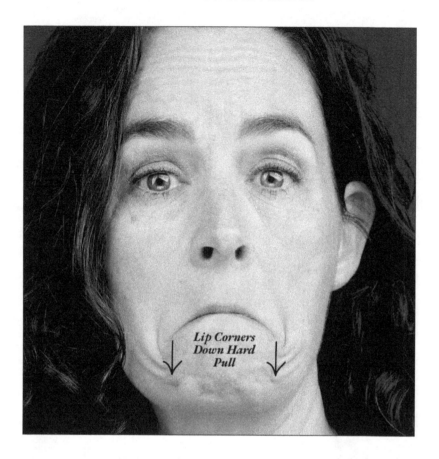

Lip Corners Down Hard Pull

17. Maybe (hmmm, will think about that)

In this closed-lipped expression, both lip corners pull down quickly and simultaneously. I often feel a slight jutting-forward of my lower jaw and teeth when I do this expression. It's a big expression rather than a fleeting one. It may express, "Hmmm, let me think about that." So if you're giving a business pitch and you see this expression, it's an indicator that you still have more work to do to convince the other person. I've also seen this expression when it means, "Wow, not bad, I'm impressed!" In that case, it's often accompanied by nodding and words that convey approval.

Guess the expression! Then turn the page. $\longrightarrow$

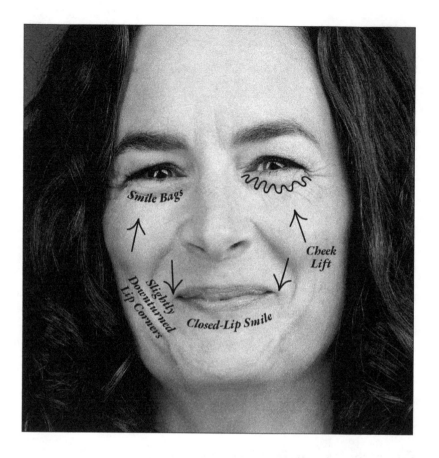

18. Mirth

In this expression, there's a *slight* downturn of both lip corners (I would also define this as "sass"—my eldest does this expression often), combined with a lift of the cheeks in pleasure that pull up a closed-lipped smile. It may also have an added slight *tricksy* element shown by a wrinkling and squishing of the nose (wrinkles on the middle part of the nose on both sides).

Guess the expression! Then turn the page. ⟶

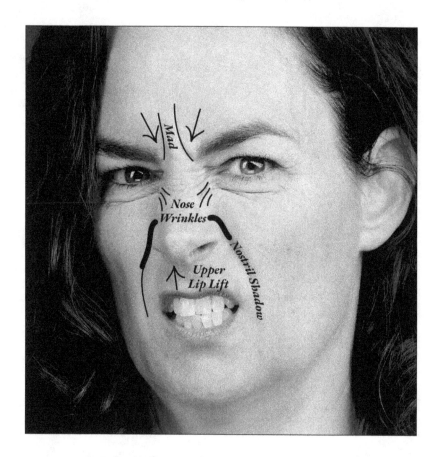

19. NO Face

This is the "Ew face," the "I'm-uncomfortable-and-don't-want-to" face. Look for the nostril shadows at the top of the nasolabial folds (the lines that run from the nostrils diagonally down to the lip corners). Sometimes the nostril shadows form a clear line that looks like upside-down fish hooks that curl around the top of the nostrils and in toward the center of the nose. This expression can also have a raised upper lip on one or both sides of the mouth—the quintessential look of disapproval that is used particularly among mean girls in the United States. The NO face also often has a "scrunched nose," with wrinkles on one or both sides of the nose.

Guess the expression! Then turn the page. ⟶

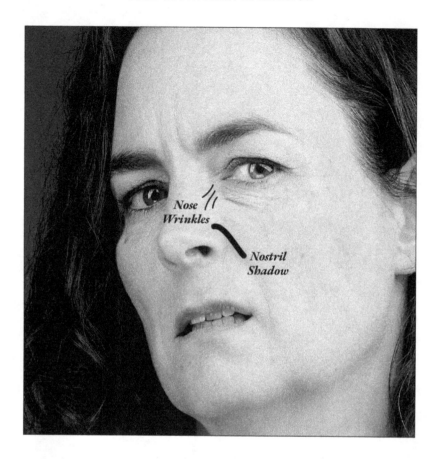

20. No (fleeting)

This is a fleeting expression of the NO Face, which has a quick jump/jolt upward of the skin on one side of the nose. This creates wrinkles next to the nose, as well as a nostril shadow and an upward pull of the lip on that side of the face. I always do this expression on the left side of my face, but this varies from person to person.

Guess the expression! Then turn the page. ⟶

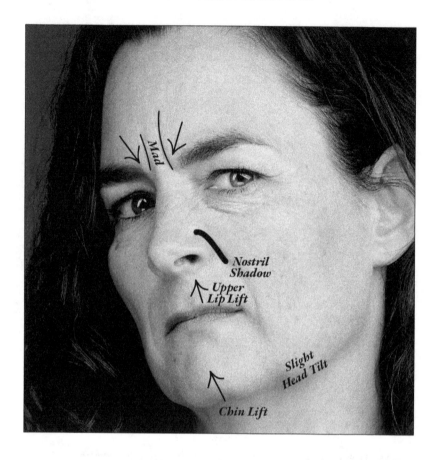

21. No (of disapproval)

This expression of disapproval includes the furrowed brow of anger, the nostril shadows and lifting of the upper lip of the NO Face, and a chin lift with a slight jut of judgment.

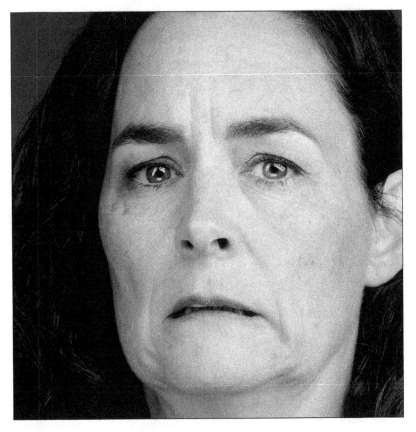

Guess the expression! Then turn the page. $\longrightarrow$

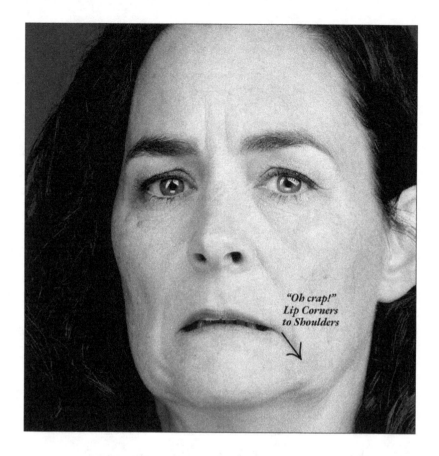

"Oh crap!"
Lip Corners
to Shoulders

22. Oh Crap!

In the "Oh Crap!" expression, one or both lip corners pull diagonally down to the respective shoulder, often accompanied by a sucking inhale (that sounds like a reverse hiss). We make this face when we receive worrying information, for example if someone gives you a deadline that you think you can't meet. If you see someone making this face when you ask for help with something, you should ask more questions to get to the bottom of what's going on. When I train people for high-stakes negotiations, especially in mergers and acquisitions, I tell them to watch for fear when asking about deliverables. If, for example, someone is saying they, "absolutely will have the product ready for market by X date," and they show fear, their face is indicating they don't actually believe what they are saying.

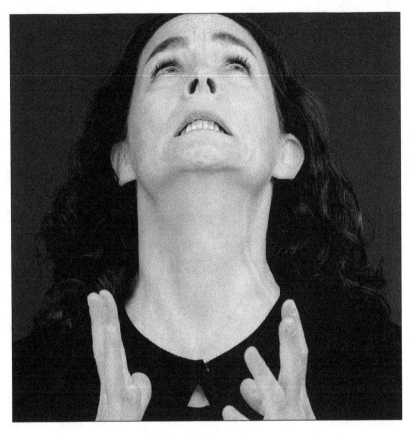

Guess the expression! Then turn the page. $\longrightarrow$

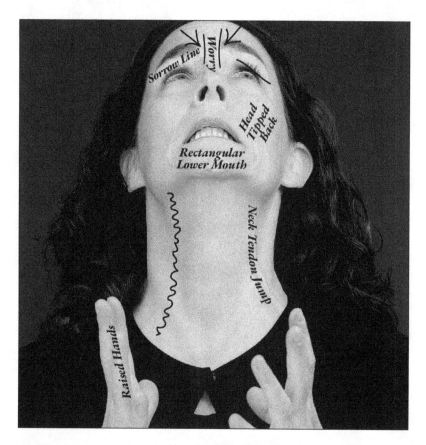

23. Pain, Anguish, Grief

Physical and emotional pain both have pieces of sadness in the raisiny chin and triangulated eyebrows, and pieces of fear in the rectangular lower lip and jump of neck tendons. Pain has an element of fear because pain not only hurts, but also *feels* permanent in the moment. Pain has a furrowed brow, showing a worried attempt to solve the problem. This complicates the expression by pulling down the inner edges of the eyebrows that are simultaneously trying to lift from sadness. The result is a chaotic, wrinkly mess with ripples going every which way. In extreme grief, there is often a lift of the head toward heaven and a raising and stretching of the hands as if praying to God. True grief is deeper than what I'm showing here, but my brain is probably relieved to not be fully immersed in the emotion—I know from experience that my body would believe the trauma message, and it would take me at least a day or two to recover.

Guess the expression! Then turn the page. $\longrightarrow$

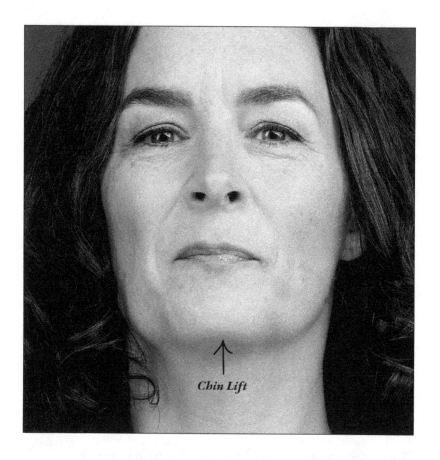

Chin Lift

24. Pride

In pride, the chin thrusts up and forward, sometimes accompanied by the lifted cheeks of joy. In this photo, I have a bit of a mirthy mouth with a close lipped smile that has the lip corners pulled slightly BOTH up and down. Defiance is similar to pride, but in addition to the chin lift, it will also have elements of other expressions, like pieces of anger, the nostril shadows of the NO Face, or the raisiny chin of vulnerability.

Guess the expression! Then turn the page. ⟶

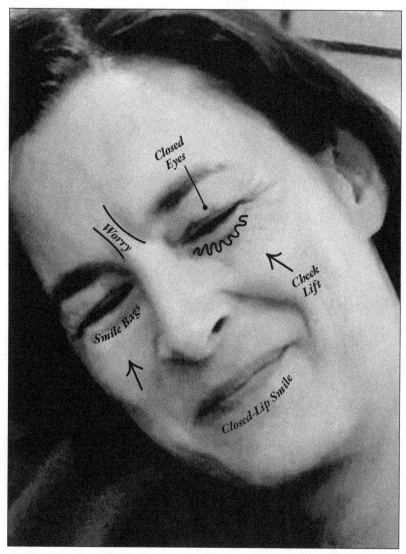

25. Relief

Relief lifts the cheeks in happiness and puckers the chin in vulnerability. In this photograph, the lines between my eyebrows are still furrowed from worry, and my eyes are shut, closing out the world to fully marinate in the emotion. The corners of my lips are pulled at once up and down, as is common in a soft, affectionate, platonic love smile. Note that worry and thinking both use the same muscle movements. I use context, including analyzing my own feelings in the moment, to differentiate between the two.

Guess the expression! Then turn the page. $\longrightarrow$

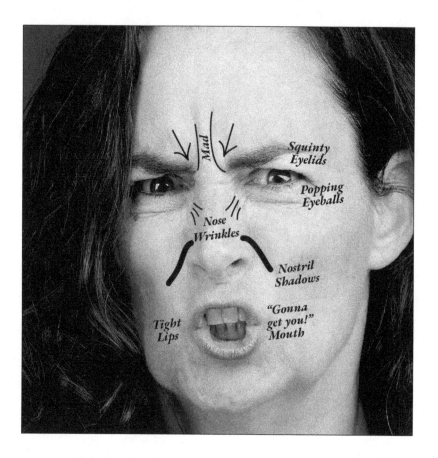

26. RUN! Face

This is a complex expression that shows that someone is ready to hurt another person. I used to demonstrate this while training my kids when they were little. No matter who made this face, my kids knew this expression meant they needed to *RUN!* because this person was likely to assault them. A furrowed brow, squinty eyelids, and popping eyeballs all show anger. The nose wrinkles, lifted lip, and nostril shadows show the NO Face. Tight lips with a "gonna get you!" mouth that reaches out toward the intended victim show extreme aggression. Try making this face and see how it makes you feel—it's truly awful.

Guess the expression! Then turn the page. $\longrightarrow$

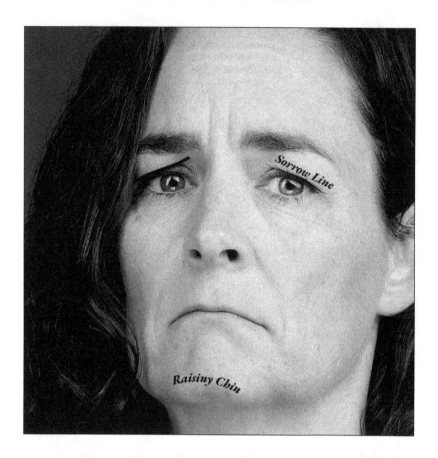

27. Sadness

The expression of sadness includes the squeezed chin of vulnerability and sorrow lines. Sorrow lines stretch from the inner eyebrows down to the outside corners of the eyelids. In sadness, the inner eyebrows often raise, although in this picture, that doesn't show because my eyebrows are furrowed slightly from worry.

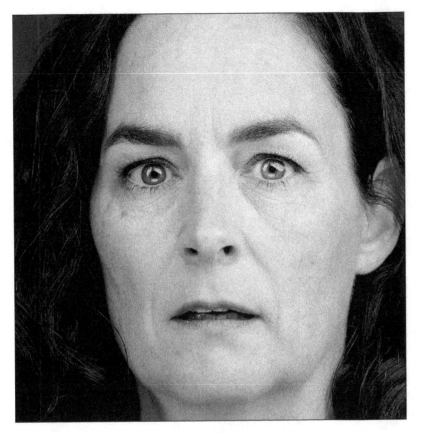

Guess the expression! Then turn the page. ⟶

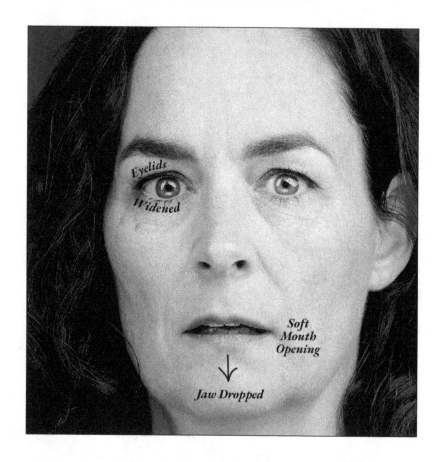

28. Surprise, Shock

Surprise differs from fear in that all its pieces are rounder. The eyebrows are softer in their "rise." The mouth and eyebrows are both "O" shaped. The chin drops and looks like the person forgot to hold their jaw shut. Shock (not shown here) has a widely stretched open mouth.

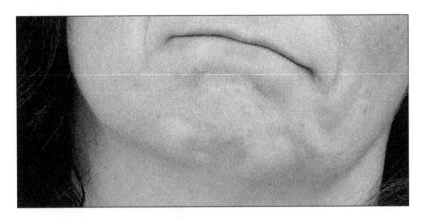

Guess the expression! Then turn the page. ⟶

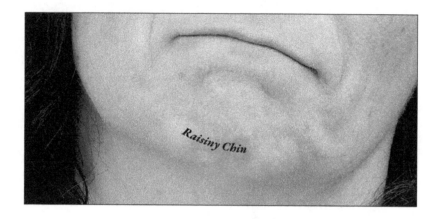

29. Vulnerability (tender)

With tender vulnerability, a squeezed chin turns the grape of the chin into a tight, dented, and puckered raisin. This creates tiny dimples, or as one of my clients says, "cellulite on the chin." This chin clench is present in **love, tenderness, empathy, and sadness**—indicating that there is a feeling of loss or the possibility of loss—"*I'm vulnerable.*" To practice this chin, first squeeze your butt muscles. Now do the same with your chin muscles. Yup, I find this funny.

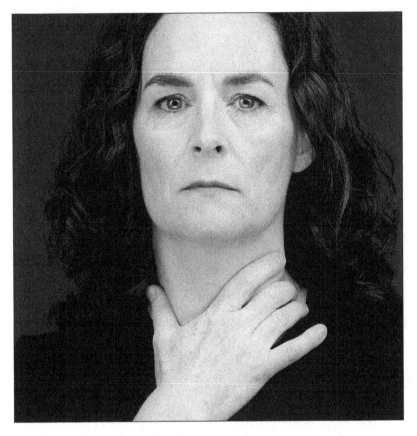

Guess the expression! Then turn the page. ⟶

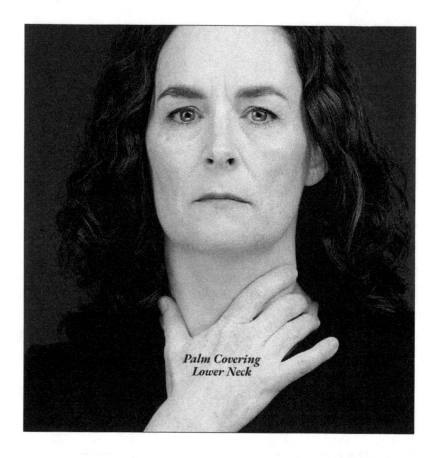

*Palm Covering
Lower Neck*

30. Vulnerability (feeling unsafe)

This is a particularly telling gesture, which I'm including because it's universal. Like all the facial expressions I teach, it exists irrespective of language, culture, upbringing, and socialization. The expression of feeling vulnerable and unsafe is shown by covering the neck with one hand.

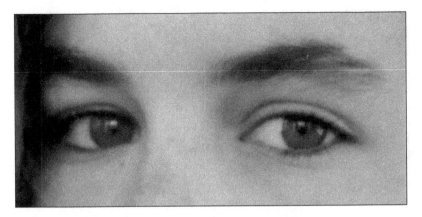

Guess the expression! Then turn the page. $\longrightarrow$

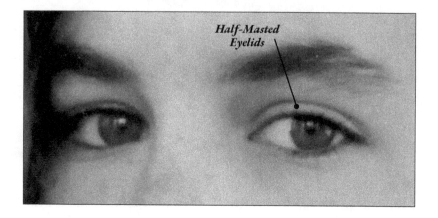

Half-Masted Eyelids

31. Want, Desire, Seduction

In romance: want, desire, and seduction are shown by lowering the eyelids straight down and half-hooding or half-masting the eyelids. In literature, we call this "bedroom eyes." Sleepy eyelids are different, and I'm still figuring that out, but the irises and pupils in sleepy eyes look much less focused and intense. The angles of the eyelids coming down is also different in sleepy eyes and not a straight drop.

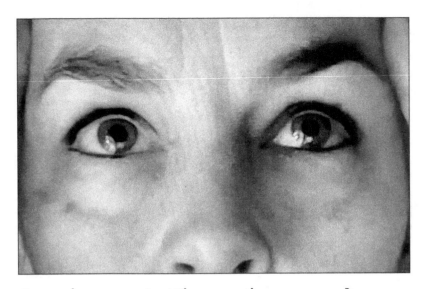

Guess the expression! Then turn the page. ⟶

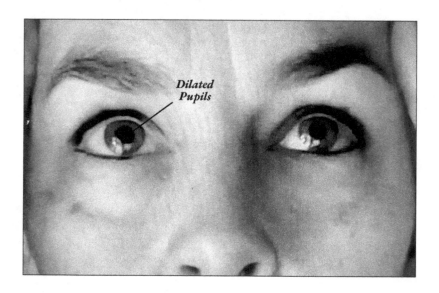

Dilated Pupils

32. Want, Greed, Desire

Want, greed, and desire are shown in the swelling of the pupils. Our pupils also dilate from other stimuli, such as light and medication. To make sure you are assessing pupil dilation correctly, look for an increase in pupil size in real-time and in response to something said, seen, or reacted to. In every encounter, I gauge how big the other person's pupils are at the *beginning* of our meeting, and then I watch to see if there is a change during our conversation. This is especially useful in business negotiations and romance. In both cases, pupil dilation is an indicator that the person is highly interested in the task at hand. Pupil dilation in business can straight-up express "Give me that!" in response to a pitch or offer. It doesn't necessarily mean attraction to another person—it can simply mean I want what you just offered (money, chocolate, status, etc.). Context is everything!

References

As is clear throughout my book, my preference when choosing terminology is more playful than scientific. This is how my brain works—it's what sticks for me, and therefore what I can teach effectively. My work and process tend toward the pragmatic rather than the scientific, and I can't imagine sitting in a laboratory conducting experiments. I do, however, love mischief and am comfortable saying something comedic and outrageous to a stranger to elicit an expression I'm "working on."

Much of what I teach comes from the years I have spent studying language after language in immersive situations. My stubborn brain decided that if I had been born in a different country, I would have spoken that language perfectly—so I believed the key to learning languages was to remove my English completely and start with a clean brain slate.

Put simply, I have spent years of my life not understanding the spoken words around me, years of using facial expressions and body language to interpret intent, years of observing facial movements and coming up with my own interpretations of what these movements meant. All the while paying attention to every jump, jolt, twist, lift, push, and squeeze on my own face. I learned to listen deeply to what my own face whispers to my brain and my heart, and I still wake from dreams in the middle of the night and freeze my face mid-expression while reaching for something to write on before the insight and expression is lost. Yes, I am strange, as humans so often are. And yes, my obsession, like many other peoples' obsessions, is born from trauma.

My children have also put their own words on expressions, and I use many of these in my teaching. Lea, Emma, and Matthias are my laboratory, and I am theirs.

All this to say, I am entirely responsible for my own interpretations and chosen vocabulary, and it is my belief that some of the things I teach significantly transgress what has been proven in the scientific community. Certainly, it is possible that others would disagree with some of the expressions I teach and the methodologies I use. And, though I do not know what others would think of my simplifications, translations, and thorough reliance on my own face and feelings to decode expressions, I do indeed lean heavily on the experts in the field of facial expressions whose work has so deeply inspired me.

Therefore, I would like to express my sincere gratitude to the behavioral scientists whose research and writings have been invaluable to me and so many others. I wouldn't be able to do much of what I do without the individuals that have dedicated decades of their lives to decoding and identifying facial muscle movements and expressions.

Each of these behavioral scientists has worked tirelessly and followed established scientific methods to put words on what was previously considered invisible or even non-existent, and each has endeavored to document, translate, and teach others.

When I give keynotes, I refer to Charles Darwin and his book, *The Expression of the Emotions in Man and Animals*, which he published in 1872. We humans are hardwired in our facial expressions, and humans have written about facial expressions for as long as humans have been writing. However, Darwin paid *particular* attention to facial expressions and took great care in categorizing and documenting them. I like to think that we both experienced some of our aha moments under the same circumstances and in the same ways, in our travels over and over to foreign lands where we didn't know the language. When language isn't accessible, the brain switches on and lights up areas of seeing and understanding that would otherwise be ignored. When that happens, eternal patterns begin to emerge.

When I've taught in church, I've called my talk, "God's Language." It is my belief that facial expressions are the foundation that God has given us upon which we build verbal languages. The words we use and the names and sounds we humans invent vary, but I believe our original, nonverbal language is God-given and holy.

Carl-Herman Hjortsjö is one of the earlier 20th-century researchers of facial expressions. Hjortsjö was a Swedish anatomist who worked at the Swedish University where I did my undergraduate and graduate degrees, the University of Lund. He was methodical in his categorization of facial expressions. I read his work a long time ago in its original Swedish but lost interest when repeated rumors surfaced that he was racist.

Over the years, I've heard many whispers about different systems and ways of categorizing facial expressions, including that some countries, law enforcement agencies, militaries, etc. have their own methods. My guess is that the field has advanced in many places and in many ways, including AI, that I don't know about. How could this not be the case, given the human thirst for knowledge and that this is the universal language of our species?

Ultimately, I view learning to read facial expressions as a teachable skill that should be accessible to young people who value kindness and who want to live connected, meaningful lives. People who want to be good at loving and protecting both others and themselves. In my heart, that's what all this is for.

Current Experts and Leaders in Facial Expressions

Thank you from the bottom of my heart to the following modern leaders in the field of facial expressions. I encourage my readers to partake in any and all books, papers, and other teachings by the following experts:

Paul Ekman, who has deeply inspired me, and who has developed the largest and, in my understanding, the most thorough body of work in the field of macro- and microexpressions. He's brilliant and specific, and he has committed his life to meticulous scientific research that he so generously shares. In my view, he has changed the world. I'm eternally grateful to him, as well as to **Wallace V. Friesen** for authoring the "Facial Action Coding System" (FACS) in 1978, and for later updating FACS in 2002 along with **Joseph Hagar**. This pioneering body of work has given scientific legitimacy and structure to the field.

David Matsumoto is an expert, researcher, and teacher of facial expressions who has made significant contributions to the field.

Finally, I would like to thank **Erika Rosenberg**, who taught me FACS. Erika is brilliant, knowledgeable, and deeply committed to teaching and moving the field forward in groundbreaking ways. Words cannot express my gratitude.

Body Language

In my experience, the people who are the very best at body language are those who have a background in the military, or CIA, FBI, MI6, etc., and who have both received high-level training *and* used these skills in life-or-death situations.

While it's certainly possible to learn these skills in other ways, body language is notoriously fiddly—making it all too easy for self-proclaimed experts to make generalizations that someone with real training and experience can poke holes in, especially someone who is multilingual and multicultural, since so many aspects of body language are *not* universal.

Years ago, when I read **Joe Navarro's** material, I remember waiting for him to get something wrong—something where I've observed the opposite in my twenty-five years of living in foreign places ... He didn't. He kept getting it right. In particular, I love what he says about lie detection, about feet and torso "tells" in body language, and about how humans self-soothe by touching their skin in different ways. If you want to learn more about body language, I recommend you start with him.

About Annie

Annie Särnblad is a preeminent global speaker and expert in reading facial expressions, as well as an esteemed strategic advisor. She has developed her own, easy-to-absorb teaching techniques for facial expressions based on the knowledge she accumulated living in nine countries and studying eight languages through immersion. She is also certified in the Facial Action Coding System (FACS).

After leaving her hometown of Glencoe, Illinois on a Rotary Scholarship at the age of sixteen, Annie spent twenty-five years living outside her native United States across Asia, Europe, and Central America. She earned a Masters in Cultural Anthropology and started her career as a strategic advisor to Fortune 500s, startups, and family offices. She spent two decades coaching CEOs and management teams and sitting in on high-stakes negotiations.

Annie's clients currently hire her as a strategic advisor and/or for microexpressions training for their businesses. She has taught workshops for 4,000+ CEOs and Managing Directors all over the globe. Her clients end up finding her coaching transformative in both their professional and personal lives.

Although Annie is certified in FACS, she doesn't use FACS in her teaching, and her methods differ greatly from those of other experts in the field of nonverbal communication. This is because much of what she learned about facial expressions and nonverbal communications stems from spending many years of her life living and working abroad, studying languages through immersion, and so often not understanding what the people around her were saying.

Her unique teaching vocabulary and methods were developed during the trial, error, and aha moments of working with her children to recognize, translate, and simplify the expressions they saw on the faces around them as they lived on three continents. Annie's obsession with teaching her children facial expressions was born from her childhood trauma and deep need to keep her kids safer than she was. Survival instincts illuminate parts of the brain that would otherwise remain dormant.

Because children learn best when learning is fun, Annie's teaching methods involve interactive elements, as well as poking, prodding, and play.

As it turns out, humans are humans, and the learning techniques that work well for kids also work delightfully well for grown adults, especially people in positions of immense power who often have little time and short attention spans.

Learn more at **anniesarnblad.com**

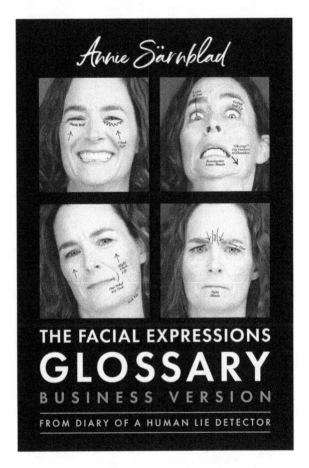